Bobby Hutcherson, 1976

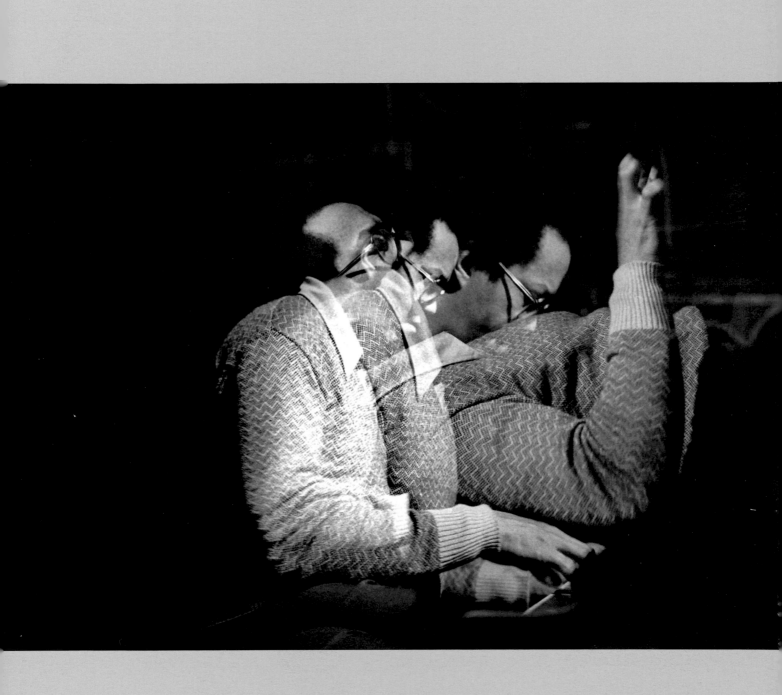

Cedar Walton, 1977

Charlie Haden, 1978

Elvin Jones, 1976

portrait of a jazz club

PHOTOGRAPHS AND INTERVIEWS BY KATHY SLOANE

Edited by Sascha Feinstein and Kathy Sloane

INDIANA UNIVERSITY PRESS *Bloomington & Indianapolis*

KEYSTONE
KORNER

This book is a publication of

INDIANA UNIVERSITY PRESS
601 North Morton Street
Bloomington, IN 47404–3797 USA

iupress.indiana.edu

Telephone orders 800-842-6796
Fax orders 812-855-7931

♾ The paper used in this publication
meets the minimum requirements of
the American National Standard for
Information Sciences–Permanence of
Paper for Printed Library Materials,
ANSI Z39.48–1992.

Manufactured in the
United States of America

*Library of Congress
Cataloging-in-Publication Data*

Sloane, Kathy, [date]
    Keystone Korner : portrait of a jazz club
/ photographs and interviews by Kathy
Sloane ; edited by Sascha Feinstein and
Kathy Sloane.
    p. cm.
ISBN 978-0-253-35691-8 (pbk. : alk.
paper)
1. Jazz – California – San Francisco – 1971–
1980 – Pictorial works. 2. Jazz – California – San Francisco – 1981–1990 – Pictorial
works. 3. Keystone Korner (Night Club :
San Francisco, Calif.) – Pictorial works.
4. Jazz musicians – California – San
Francisco – Interviews. 5. San Francisco
(Calif.) – Social life and customs – 20th
century – Pictorial works. I. Feinstein,
Sascha, 1963– II. Title. III. Title: Keystone
Corner.
    ML3508.8.S26S56   2012
    792.709794'61 – dc23
                                    2011030458

1 2 3 4 5   17 16 15 14 13 12

In honor of my parents, Perry J. and Neddie Sloane,

and

for my daughter, Ayisha Basha Knight-Shaw

I was there. I had a camera. I had a passion and the joyous chance to dwell in the sounds and sights of jazz at Keystone Korner. I hope these images and interviews suggest both the vitality of those years and my gratitude to the musicians who taught me so much while giving me great pleasure.

KEYSTONE KORNER presents
MILES DAVIS

SAT., APRIL 20, 1974 · 11:30 p.m.

ADMIT ONE
Good for 1 show only Adm. $7.00

No. 095

Joseph Jarman, 1981

CONTENTS

Ahmad Jamal, 1977

Laurie Antonioli	*singer; director, vocal jazz studies, The Jazzschool, Berkeley, California*
Todd Barkan	*owner, Keystone Korner; record producer; programming director, Dizzy's Club Coca Cola at Jazz at Lincoln Center*
Carl Burnett	*drummer (Abdul Karim Salih)*
George Cables	*pianist*
Billy Harper	*saxophonist*
Ora Harris	*cook, Keystone Korner; artist manager*
Eddie Henderson	*trumpeter*
Terri Hinte	*public relations director, Fantasy Records; freelance writer, editor, publicist*
Jack Hirschman	*writer; San Francisco Poet Laureate*
Orrin Keepnews	*record producer; founder, Riverside, Milestone, and Landmark record companies; NEA jazz master*
Calvin Keys	*guitarist*
Maria Rosa Keys	*teacher*
Stuart Kremsky	*Monday night soundman, Keystone Korner; archivist, Fantasy Records*
David Liebman	*saxophonist; NEA jazz master*
devorah major	*writer; teacher; San Francisco Poet Laureate*
Eddie Marshall	*drummer*
Ronnie Matthews	*pianist*
Flicka McGurrin	*waitress, Keystone Korner; owner, Pier 23 Restaurant and Club; painter*
John Ross	*writer; revolutionary*
Bob Stewart	*tuba player*
Steve Turre	*trombonist; shells player*
David Williams	*bassist*
Helen Wray	*waitress, Keystone Korner; landscape designer*
Al Young	*writer; teacher; California Poet Laureate*

Al Young

Al Young

The spirit of communality and self-expression lives at the heart center of jazz and blues, as well as many vernacular and classical musical traditions. While we tend to view self-expression as purely individual expression, we do so at the risk of forgetting how tightly we're plugged into everyone and everything else going on around us. As Charles Mingus stated more than once: "You have to improvise on something. You can't improvise on nothing."

Before and during the Prohibition era of the early twentieth century, San Francisco had its honky-tonks, speakeasies, barrelhouses, and jazz joints. Tom Stoddard's brilliant, painstakingly researched *Jazz on the Barbary Coast* tracks and tells the story and doesn't leave out Jelly Roll Morton's short-lived Jupiter Club, which bumped and jumped in North Beach at Jackson and Kearney in the 1920s. But in the nested history of San Francisco jazz clubs, taverns, cabarets, and bars that have blazed and flickered since Barbary Coast days, Keystone Korner truly stands out.

All heart and guts, Todd Barkan, Keystone Korner's savvy visionary and uncanny owner, never enjoyed the kind of big-time, official backing the Port of Oakland now provides for Yoshi's – once one of Keystone's exciting underdog East Bay rivals – yet he somehow managed to hold the 200-seat club together for more than a decade, usually on a shoestring budget and sometimes on a no-string budget. In its cash-strapped lifetime, the club was on financial life support and yet remained artistically healthy for years, one night at a time, one set at a time. During the ride, Keystone Korner inspired and provided the setting for a superb library of live jazz albums, as documented in this book's discography. Moreover, Keystone's laid-back ambiance drew players, visitors, and acolytes from all over the world. Stan Getz once called it "the number one jazz club in the world today." Singer-lyricist Jon Hendricks described Keystone as "the finest jazz club in the Bay Area and fast becoming one of the most important cultural institutions in the world." Premier pianists McCoy Tyner and Cecil Taylor – and so many other important artists – expressed similarly passionate affection.

The energy of Keystone even reached me when I was many miles away, a visiting writer at the University of Washington. National Public Radio used to broadcast a live show from Keystone as part of its New Year's celebration of the nation's jazz clubs. One broadcast I fondly revisit on cassette tape sweeps me back to Seattle, December 31, 1979, where – snug and warm on that cold, rainy night in a big rented house in Windermere, a gated community – my little family and I soaked up the sound of "music from home." (I borrow that phrase from the title of a book of poems by Seattle-based Colleen McElroy, the Sarah Vaughan of poets.) At the stroke of midnight, Art Blakey and his tireless Jazz Messengers bopped out a stirring version of "Auld Lang Syne," which let me hear again how much of the Scots Irish folk tradition jazz has absorbed and adopted.

"Art Blakey is one of the few living schools of this music," Todd Barkan told jazz scholar-producer Herb Wong in 1978. "When he comes to town, everyone at Keystone Korner – including the bartenders, wait-resses, and managers – feels the promise and purpose of the club [are] fulfilled and we realize why we knock ourselves out week after week." Having dwelled six months in Seattle, I'd gotten so homesick for the Bay Area that I grew wistful, even a little tearful, picturing myself back home at Keystone Korner to ring in 1980. In some ways, feeling like this made no sense. After all, my home base then was Palo Alto, one hour south of San Francisco. "Home" was another rented house, not a jazz club, and by then, of course, jazz had emigrated so globally that it could no longer call any particular place home.

I had gone through a similar sea change in Paris years before, when I and my girlfriend, whom I would soon marry, got to the Blue Note in Paris – and who should we find there but saxophonist Johnny Griffin, playing Thelonious Monk's "Rhythm-a-ning" on alien soil. The joyful sound of it carried me from France, where they called such joints *boîtes* and *caves*, back to New York and the first clubs that allowed me entry: Birdland, the Half Note, the Village Vanguard, the Village Gate, the Five Spot, the Jazz Gallery, Eddie Condon's.

But this 1979 New Year's air shot of Art Blakey and the Messen-gers – featuring Valery Ponomarev, Bobby Watson, and David Schnit-ter, a group that had already made *In This Korner*, the first of three Keystone albums by the Jazz Messengers – made me homesick. How ludicrous and heartfelt! How blue can you get?

Keystone sat at 750 Vallejo; the substation precinct known as the North Beach Police Station stood at 766 Vallejo. Jazz and fuzz.

"Whazzup with that?" I still hear my son Michael ask. Then again, how could I forget Lem Winchester, the gifted Wilmington, Delaware, police officer and vibraphonist? Winchester was a cop who embraced jazz wholly, taking the great Milt Jackson as his model, then veering offbeat in his own after-hours directions. His beautiful tune "Down Fuzz" from *Winchester Special* smoothed and comforted me on many a tangled night before I escaped into my thirties.

I would often see cops parked in front of the club or patrolling the intersection on foot. What were they feeling or thinking as they took in the music? A jazz club jammed up next to a police station seemed perfectly normal – or perhaps paranormal – to me. This was how reality worked. How could a child of the '50s and '60s come to any other conclusion? Irony reigned. "Scrap irony," I called it. Like matter and antimatter, poetry and anti-poetry, or insiders and outsiders, hipsters and squares balanced things out. *If you think the police are so bad,* a popular bumper sticker of the day declared, *the next time somebody breaks into your house, call a hippie!* Deep down, I loved the paradox. Keystone Korner drew its first and last breath in a mix-and-match era whose avant-garde byword was "everything is everything." Cops and crooks have always played against and need one another – that was clear enough, even then – but now that this music, once regarded as disreputable, had gone legit, what was all the fuss and chase about?

I enjoy imagining how Freddie Herrera, the original owner and anointer of Keystone Korner, contemplated the club's name: "Okay, so there's a police precinct next door. Why not let's make the best of this? 'Keystone,' that's what we'll call it. We'll name it after the Keystone Kops" – director Mack Sennett's doofus pie-throwing screw-ups of silent two-reeler fame, whose herky-jerky antics packed movie palaces between 1912 and 1917. Freddie Herrera, like Todd Barkan, might have remembered watching prints of those jumpy, preposterous screen cops on a high-speed chase in the wake of some crime when, *whoops,* the car's steering wheel comes off!

In 1970, when you named a place Keystone, you automatically got the buzzword *stone* tossed in. This was key. The Rolling Stones already had introduced themselves as "the world's greatest rock & roll band," and Sly and the Family Stone were hot on the scene, big time. The Fifth Dimension was hitting the charts with Laura Nyro's "Stoned Soul Picnic"; Bob Dylan's "Like a Rolling Stone" and Ray Charles' "Let's Go Get Stoned" had already become keepsakes. And the chunky newsstand tabloid known as *Rolling Stone,* for which I was a steady book reviewer, thrived.

Just before he sold the original Keystone Korner to Todd Barkan in July 1972 for $12,500, Freddie Herrera featured such acts as Elvin Bishop, Mike Bloomfield, Jerry Garcia, and Merl Saunders. After he sold Keystone Korner, Herrera acquired the New Monk, a tiny rock-friendly club on Berkeley's University Avenue across the Bay, close to the UC campus. Herrera then changed the name to Keystone Berkeley. In no time, up sprang Keystone Palo Alto, where rock, zydeco, bluegrass, jazz, blues, and punk rotated. Then up jumped the downtown San Francisco rock-and-pop Broadway venue known as the Stone. And for me, all of it floated back to the 1940s, when ethnomusicologist Alan Lomax carried his portable 78 rpm Library of Congress disk recorder to capture a future blues legend, who was still sharecropping under the name McKinley Morganfield at the Stovall Plantation on the Mississippi Delta: Muddy Waters, and his shiveringly haunting "Rolling Stone."

Rock was coming on strong around that time and having a profound influence on jazz. When Warner Brothers asked me to write the liner notes for George Benson's *Breezin'*, they sent me the very basic tracks – just George Benson and the rhythm section, without the overdubbed string sections – and I could hear clearly that Benson was doing what jazz musicians have always done with the music surrounding them. Jazz is an idiom into which all kinds of musical formats can be processed. Popular music, classical music, folk stuff, whatever. You can rag or klezmerize or jazz the classics. Whenever you get musical neighbors living around one another, it's inevitable that they're going to rub more than shoulders. And at Keystone Korner, especially before Todd Barkan took over, there were collaborations between musicians – Merl Saunders and Jerry Garcia, for example – who performed jazz-flavored rock. They were leaning toward each other.

But Todd Barkan wanted a recognizably "pure" jazz menu, and most of the musicians who played at Keystone preferred that as well. I'm reminded of a night in the mid-sixties at the Jazz Workshop (Keystone didn't exist yet) and the tone in Rahsaan Roland Kirk's voice when he complained about the rock and British invasion. Rahsaan decided to test those of us in the audience. He was complaining that one of his A&R men wanted him to jazz up some Beatles tunes and rock material.

"What do y'all think about that?" he asked.

"No, Roland," we shot back at once. "Tell them to kiss your ass."

"That's what I told them."

Perhaps I should set up the jazz environment that preceded Keystone. I arrived in San Francisco for the first time in 1960 and promptly found my way to Berkeley on the F bus. The fare back then was fifty cents. Settling in following my second arrival less than a year later, I became one of those tedious Bay Areans who didn't feel compelled to go over to San Francisco to hear jazz. There was plenty of the stuff in the East Bay. Besides, I was living on nickels, dimes, quarters, and one-dollar bills.

I remember the Trois Couleurs in Oakland, named after France's own red, white, and blue. Trois Couleurs was owned by Cuz Cousineau, a drummer and vibist who recorded with Paul Desmond in 1950, and who also deejayed with me at radio station KJAZ, when it had studios in Berkeley at Telegraph and Russell. Right next door to the tiny station, the club Tsubo sprang up in 1961. The owner, Glenn Ross, modeled his no-alcohol club-restaurant after those seriously intellectual jazz coffeehouses he had frequented and grown to love during his tenure as an expatriate in Tokyo during the 1950s. Sometimes while I was on the air at KJAZ, the sound from the Tsubo bandstand seeped through the thinly insulated walls. Listeners got in on the live session that produced the 1962 Wes Montgomery album, *Full House*, with Johnny Griffin and the Miles Davis rhythm section of Wynton Kelly, Paul Chambers, and Jimmy Cobb. Tsubo shut down in mid-October 1962, after only eighteen months. Then the Jabberwock, poet Belle Randall's Alice-in-Wonderland folk club, took over.

Across the Golden Gate Bridge in exotic Sausalito, pianist Vince Guaraldi – now famous for the scores he composed for the Peanuts TV specials in general and for the songs "Lucy and Linus" and "Christmas Time Is Near" in particular – used to broadcast live from the Trident. We carried his Saturday night show over KJAZ. Just then, in 1962, Guaraldi was pushing "Cast Your Fate to the Wind," a number that would become his first international signature hit and find its way onto his big-selling Fantasy album: *Jazz Impressions of Black Orpheus*.

Still, San Francisco pulled and won us over. Excitement burned the air like ozone. On Broadway alone, you slammed into jazz galore. There was the now-famous Jazz Workshop. Directly across the street was Sugar Hill, singer Barbara Dane's club, where whispery ballad master Ben Webster played his last stateside gig before taking up permanent residence in Europe. Down by a Bay Bridge connection that got wiped out in the Loma Prieta earthquake of 1989, Basin Street West popped up. Then, after Sugar Hill dissolved, El Matador not so much replaced it as conquered Broadway. It booked pricey artists. Whenever Oscar Peterson played there, Clint Eastwood showed up and columnist Herb

Caen, who coined the word *beatnik*, briskly reported it. Singer Anita O'Day signed a vinyl album for me at El Matador, then went home downstate to Century City to find that her home had gone up in smoke. For me, at least, the club's air seemed mysterious, if not arrogant and secretive; El Matador intrigued me. The club would close whenever its owners felt like it. At Thanksgiving, for example, a sign would appear in the window that said, more or less: "El Matador will be closed until January. Have a great holiday." You didn't mess with the bartending manager; he was packing. If I handed the waitress a $20 bill, she would give me change for a ten. I'd have to argue with her *and* the guy with the gun in order to get my change.

Jazz turned up all around North Beach, especially in little places. As an active folksinger who sang plenty of blues in 1963, I worked in one of those little places: the Coffee Gallery on Green Street. On its jazz nights – but only in my poet mind – Green Street became Green Dolphin Street. Saxophonist Pony Poindexter used to play the Coffee Gallery behind Bev Kelly, whom I remember as a sexy blonde vocalist. When the strip clubs first came in, some of the local jazz musicians worked the strip joints and then sat in after-hours at the jazz clubs. And, of course, the Cellar was still going when I first reached the city. Famous for its spoken-word nights in the 1950s, the Cellar kicked off that decade's poetry and jazz craze. Beat poets like Lawrence Ferlinghetti, Allen Ginsberg, Kenneth Patchen, and Kenneth Rexroth held forth and flourished. Everything I was interested in – music, books, painting, theater, comedy, politics, cultural craziness – kept leading me to North Beach. Before I settled in California, it had been New York's Greenwich Village and nearby Mott Street. In both locales, Italian and Asian cultures touched. If there is anything to the legend, Marco Polo's journey to Cathay might have had something to do with this.

Keystone Korner emerged at a time when those frequenting rock clubs eclipsed the jazz audiences. In addition, hard bop, Keystone's idiom of choice, was fast becoming conservatory music as jazz education moved from bandstands into college classrooms. Indeed, by the time Todd Barkan took over Keystone Korner in 1972, just about all the jazz clubs in the Bay Area had closed, leaving people like me thirsty and grateful for the music we loved.

Just as some people harbor the notion that meat, eggs, milk, cheese, fruits, vegetables, bread, and cereals all come from the grocery store, many visitors to jazz clubs take it on faith that music, musicians, and nightclubs simply emerge as the night blooms and ripens. Storytellers and poets know better. Behind everything we live with, there's a story. The story of Keystone Korner is so complex that it's comforting to have Kathy Sloane's photographs and pages in hand to allow me to revisit and sample a tiny portion of my own plate of Keystone memories, as well as some reflective thoughts about jazz clubs worldwide.

I read about jazz clubs, for example, long before I ever set foot in one. Then, during spring break of 1957, I hitched a ride with college friends from Ann Arbor, Michigan, to New York City. I was a seventeen-year-old jazz nerd – impatient, on fire. Our destination: Birdland, known worldwide as "the jazz corner of the world." Named after the brilliant saxophonist Charlie "Yardbird" Parker, Birdland glistened on Broadway west of Fifty-Second Street. You went downstairs, where the hostile, three-foot-nine Pee Wee Marquette would collect the $1.50 admission, then eyeball you for seating. "Put this boy in the peanut gallery," he always piped when he looked up at me. I didn't know it at the time, but Bird himself had already been eighty-sixed (banned or barred) from Birdland. Like I say: scrap irony.

Because Birdland's management had sense enough to rope off a section for hopeful, underage patrons, the legendary club was already dabbling in what later came to be labeled "audience development." I mention this because, as decades dissolved, I watched jazz clubs reflexively exclude listeners and fans not yet old enough to drink legally. I often think of a phrase that tenor saxophonist Archie Shepp tossed off in a *DownBeat* interview, explaining how he, a creative artist, felt when he was forced to see himself as "an adjunct to the sale of whiskey." When Todd Barkan decided to open a kitchen at Keystone Korner, his idea was to make the club friendly and accessible to minors, who could then lawfully patronize an establishment that served food. It was Birdland's "peanut gallery" insight all over again.

The management and patrons of Keystone never treated musicians as mere adjuncts to food or liquor sales, and the musicians really responded to their respect, both musically and verbally. I was right there at Keystone Korner the night Illinois Jacquet was holding forth, playing his heart out and telling us between numbers what life had been like for him as a youthful tenor saxophonist with Lionel Hampton's band. "I probably had eighty-five cents in my pocket," he began. Then Jacquet told us how the signature solo he blew on "Flying Home" just came to him, naturally, in the moment; how, after the record hit the rhythm-and-blues charts, he had sense enough to memorize his own solo, with Hamp egging him on. Jacquet's solo became so famous that crowds would sing aloud along with him as he blew. All he had to do was throw in a little honking and squealing with plenty of additional onstage theatrics and sound effects, much of it delivered on bended knee and baptized in limelight.

Some of my other favorite Keystone memories are spread out among the recollections of others in this marvelous oral history: the night Bobby Hutcherson, for example, entranced a woman with his vibraphone. But it's the spirit of Keystone that should reach out to the majority of the people reading this book – which is to say, those who never experienced the club firsthand but who can appreciate its importance as a vital West Coast venue for jazz, as the location of important recordings, and, more generally, as the embodiment of yet another unique moment in America's history.

Making itself up as it went along, Keystone Korner, like the music it presented, reinvented itself nightly, improvising mightily, bravely navigating the moment the way any tightrope walker must when she's working without a net. Given the ongoing, magnificent presence Keystone Korner has retained, I have no doubt that lovers of jazz all over the world will welcome this lush pillow-book of reminiscences and deeply felt images.

Rahsaan Roland Kirk, Steve Turre, 1977

Steve Turre

My parents took me to see Duke Ellington at the Oakland Auditorium in 1956 or '57, the year I started playing the trombone. Boy, what a memory! Ella Fitzgerald was the guest vocalist, Coleman Hawkins was a guest soloist, Clark Terry was in the band, Harry Carney, Johnny Hodges, everybody. It was amazing. It made me want to play this music. Duke was one of my heroes. My mom and dad met at a Count Basie dance at Treasure Island, so I'm here indirectly 'cause of Count Basie.

North Beach was the happening [place] of jazz. They had the Jazz Workshop, which is where I first played with Rahsaan [Roland Kirk], and I saw Sonny Rollins there; oh man, that blew my mind. They had Basin Street West, El Matador, where Oscar Peterson used to always play, and the Blackhawk. And then right around the corner was Caesar's Latin Palace; I used to go there, too. This was around '66 or '67.

Then North Beach kind of faded and the Both/And was the preeminent jazz club in San Francisco. And, of course, I saw everybody there: Miles, Cannonball, Monk, Lee Morgan, Hugh Masekela. McCoy [Tyner], when he had just left Trane, with his first trio. The Jazz Communicators: Freddie Hubbard, Joe Henderson, Cedar Walton, Louis Hayes, and Herbie Lewis. That was a killer group. Yusef Lateef. The Both/And was *the* joint. Since I played in the house band with Bishop Norman Williams, they always let me in there, so it was like school.

When the Both/And was winding down, Keystone Korner took up the slack. And then Keystone Korner became the preeminent jazz spot on the West Coast.

Carl Burnett

When [Sonny Murray] came to the Both/And club, I was living at the Happy House in San Francisco on Oak Street with a bunch of musicians. I moved there when I joined Cal Tjader in '62 or '63, and I lived there for five years. Flip Nunez was there, as were Monk Montgomery, Noel Jewkes, Clarence Becton, and others.

We had another room where traveling musicians stayed. And if anyone was gone, then different people stayed there. I was playing with Cal Tjader at the Matador, which was right across the street from the

Jazz Workshop, so at break time you could hear Thelonious Monk, Miles Davis, Cannonball Adderley. I think the first time I ever heard Flip Wilson was there.

There were after-hours places, and people went out to hear the music. That was like New York. I remember one New Year's when there were so many people they had to stop traffic. People just walked down the middle of the street. That could have never happened in L.A.

By the time Keystone opened, it was the only place that had a feeling of community – the only place that was even making an effort to bring in jazz artists. And the ones that they were bringing in, not only could you go to see and enjoy [them], but you could talk to [them]. It was like an oasis because all the other places were gone.

Sascha Feinstein
Courtesy of Divia Feinstein, 2010

Sascha Feinstein

I enjoy imagining jazz clubs as I listen to live recordings, and if those sessions took place at venues I've known, I find it downright difficult *not* to recreate (and sometimes relive) the setting. I'm thinking now of Bradley's in New York, with its long bar to the right and the portrait of Paul Desmond over his donated grand piano; when I hear recordings from Bradley's – especially the two marvelous CDs by Kenny Barron – I'm suddenly on a bar stool. Same for the Village Vanguard: I'm subterranean, surrounded by jazz portraits along the dark walls of fame. Even Carnegie Hall and festivals at Newport bring to mind specific spaces and images. Yes, the music must always be paramount and few recordings capture the energized vitality of live performance, but the ambiance of jazz creates a still greater intimacy with the music, and that's where photographs and the written word can inspire specific memories or imagined stage settings.

Like most East Coast jazz fans of my generation, I never had the opportunity to experience Keystone Korner, and until I met Kathy Sloane, I appreciated the club exclusively for its live recordings. Some of my early LP purchases included Art Blakey's *In This Korner*, McCoy Tyner's *Atlantis*, and Stan Getz's *The Dolphin*; later, I picked up astonishing Keystone recordings by Bill Evans, Dexter Gordon, Freddie Hubbard, Rahsaan Roland Kirk, Tete Montoliu, Woody Shaw, Zoot Sims, Eddie "Cleanhead" Vinson, Mary Lou Williams, Denny Zeitlin, and many others. Long before this project began, my Keystone collection had swelled – out of admiration not for the club but for its musicians. Todd Barkan's taste in music fed my musical desires; my life would be truly diminished had he not had the vision to create this club and the intelligence to record the lasting music by the artists who passed through.

And now, thanks to Kathy's photographs and her hard-earned triumph of oral history, I experience Keystone Korner all the more intimately. Sure, it's far-fetched to say that I can smell Ora's cooking when I hear the tunes, but, with ease, I can now place the sound within the psychedelic atmosphere: the tightly packed crowds awash in legal and illegal smoke, eyes focused on the musicians onstage beneath the dramatic mural. Because of the stories of the witnesses and the beautiful visuals, I listen with new ears to the introductions by such favorite artists as Dexter Gordon. "On our last European tour, we happened to visit Scotland," he announces on the first of three Keystone volumes. "We saw the – " and here he pauses with a typically long Dexter cadence, and in the background one can hear the *clink* of glasses. Suddenly, I'm wondering if it's Helen Wray, struggling with one of those weighted trays, working hard to get the drinks out before the music begins. Then Dexter hits the punch line: "Loch Ness monster." There's laughter, and someone says, "All right," as in, "Okay, if you say so." And I might as well be in the first row, looking up at this tenor genius beneath a halo of mural as he adds, "He made quite an impression."

Because the sound engineers left the tapes running, we get to hear Zoot Sims and company calling out the next tune and key ("I'll Remember April" in G) during the applause. We hear the audience whooping when Eddie "Cleanhead" Vinson starts to sing "They Call Me Mr. Cleanhead" and, later, giggling and hollering like a rent-party audience as he works his way into the climax of "Back Door Blues." On Art Pepper's *San Francisco Samba*, we hear an audience member over the final, fading notes to "Art Meets Mr. Beautiful" call to his hero, "Love you, Art." Now, with this book, we can almost befriend the audience members. For me, at least, the Keystone's doors have reopened.

Imagine, for a moment, the young bassist Marc Johnson beneath the giant mandala, his eyes half shut, almost rolled back. Drummer Joe La Barbera's to the right of the stage, and to Marc's left, behind the piano, sits their leader, Bill Evans. During a week-long engagement in 1980, the trio played several versions of "Nardis." Early in the week, Evans looked through the smoke and said, "We're going to conclude this set with an extended version of something that's been in our repertoire from the beginning. . . . We've learned from the potential of the tune, and every once in a while a new gateway opens. It's like therapy, this tune." On September 8, the last night of the engagement, the trio closes with another version of "Nardis," almost twenty minutes long. "We've had a very nice engagement here," he tells the crowd. "You people in the audiences have been wonderful, and I hope we'll be back soon." On September 15, he died.

Depending on the music, the crowds could be raucous or reverent – like congregations in disparate church settings. During a gig led by pianist Tete Montoliu, one can hear sporadic, gospel-like shouts of encouragement during Herbie Lewis's lengthy bass solo on "I'll Remember April," a twelve-and-a-half-minute tune that concludes with

"All right! All right!" and whistles and cheers. Then, Tete Montoliu relaxes the room with a rubato performance of "You've Changed." In the background, the clinking of glasses fuses with Billy Higgins's cymbals. But at a recording by Mary Lou Williams – look at Kathy's photos for a moment – she holds the crowd the way she must have entranced her college students: "Thank you. Good evening, friends. I'd like to bring you up to date to demonstrate the history of jazz. Most Americans do not know that the greatest art in the world was created in America. First was the spirituals, ragtime, Kansas City swing; that was a great era of jazz, of the well-trained musicians. Out of that: Charlie Parker, Dizzy Gillespie, Thelonious Monk – the bop era. What we're trying to do is bring good jazz back to you – with the healing in it and the spiritual feeling – so I'd like to start out with the spirituals."

In the liner notes for Rahsaan Roland Kirk's album *Bright Moments*, Joel Dorn describes the Keystone atmosphere as a "hipness that permeates the room that cannot be designed or wished into or added onto a club. It's either there or it isn't." Thanks to these oral histories, I feel that much closer to the hip environment – and all the more disappointed not to have experienced Keystone firsthand.

With Kathy's photographs, however, I can visualize the stage as I listen to these musicians speak and play, and I can feel at least an approximation of the Keystone ambiance, which seems to have been an oasis in its time and now is nearly mythic. And I can feel the deep, heartfelt honesty in Rahsaan Roland Kirk's voice when he says: "You know it's good to be in a place that feels like you in your house, you know?" (The audience responds like gospel churchgoers: "*Yeah!*") "Now, it's a beautiful thing – we glad you people are assembled here with us on this Saturday night." (Someone says, "All right.") "You know what I mean?" ("*Yeah.*" "Yeah.") "You don't feel like Saturday night people; some Saturday night people, that's the only night they get out, and they act like it." [Laughter and clapping and some mild whoops] "You know like, when you cage somethin' up and when it gets out they act like it. That's the way most Saturday night people act. Now, we would like to think of some very beautiful bright moments." ("Yeah.") "You know what I mean?" ("Yeah." "*Yeah.*") "Bright moments." ("Bright moments.") "Bright moments is like – [Rahsaan chuckles] – eatin' your last pork chop in London, England, because you ain't gonna get no mo' – " [Laughter] ("Bright moments.") " – cooked from home." ("Bright moments.") "Bright moments is like bein' with your favorite love, and y'all sharin' the same ice cream dish – [Laughter] – and you get mad when she gets the last drop." (The crowd laughs, and Rahsaan laughs with them. "Bright moments!") "And you have to take her in your arms and get it the *other* way." ("Wooo!" "Bright moments.") "Bright moments." ("Bright moments.") "That's too heavy for most of y'all because y'all don't know about that kind of love. The love y'all have been taught about is the love in those magazines, and I am fortunate that I didn't have to look in magazines." [Rahsaan laughs with the audience] "Bright moments!" ("Bright moments.") "Bright moments is like seein' somethin' that you ain't never seen in your life and you don't have to see it but you know how it looks." [Applause] ("Bright moments!" "Bright moments.") "Bright moments is like hearin' some music that ain't nobody else heard, and if they heard it they wouldn't even recognize that they heard it because they been hearin' it all their life but they nutted on it, so when you hear it and you start poppin' your feet and jumpin' up and down, they get mad because you enjoying yourself but those are bright moments that they can't share with you because they don't know . . . how to even go about listenin' to what you listenin' to, and when you try to tell 'em about it, they don't know a damn thing about what you talkin' about." [Screams, whoops, charged applause] "Is there any other bright moments before we proceed on?" ("Testify!") "Testify!" "Bright moments!" And then someone in the audience answers the calling: "Bright moments is sitting at the Keystone Korner –" ("Beautiful!") " – and listening to geniuses like Rahsaan Roland Kirk." "Beautiful. Bright moments. Bright moments. Bright moments is like havin' brothers and sisters, and sisterettes and brotherettes like y'all here listening to us." [Wild applause]

Man, I'm there. And you're there with me, aren't you?

I just wanted to present the best music that we could with the warmest feeling that we could.
Todd Barkan

Todd Barkan

Keystone Korner was, as much as anything else, the only real psychedelic jazz club that lasted. There were a couple of little experiments in that area, and isolated experiments in the United States, but Keystone was a bona fide psychedelic jazz club that emerged out of the post-psychedelic era in San Francisco – right out of flower children and Haight-Ashbury.

I was born in Lincoln, Nebraska, in 1946 and was deeply immersed in jazz from my earliest remembered times. My family moved to Columbus, Ohio, where my grandparents were, and we had lots of jazz records in the house. I listened to jazz and became a jazz fanatic by the time I was eight or nine years old. I had literally thousands of records by the time I was in college. I used to work as a construction worker and would take every penny I had and buy jazz records. And I used to hear as much jazz as I could. I first started playing the piano when I was six years old. And it was in Columbus that I met Rahsaan Roland Kirk, who became a mentor to me later on.

Ohio used to have a lot more live jazz than it has now. Miles Davis, Cannonball Adderley, Jimmy Smith – all these groups played in Ohio. It was part of the circuit: Youngstown, Columbus, Cleveland, Cincinnati, Toledo, Indianapolis, Chicago, Buffalo, Rochester. They used to play for a week or two in Columbus. It's not part of a circuit any more, so when people come through, they play for one day. Cannonball Adderley would play for a week at the Club 502. You'd have a triple bill of the John Coltrane Quartet, B. B. King, and Edwin Double-O Soul Starr. You'd have an R&B and a blues and a jazz artist all on the same bill, playing three sets a night each, from eight at night until four in the morning. It was a different era.

I went to Oberlin College, and then I went west. I was heavily into *Paladin*, the television show with Richard Boone, so I kind of went

Todd Barkan

west looking for Paladin and dreams of psychedelia. And I wound up in San Francisco, 1967, during the summer of love, with a flower in my hair and a Fender Rhodes piano, playing in an Afro-Cuban band called Kwane and the Kwandidos. It was a great band. An electric piano, Fender Rhodes, three horns. John Handy played in that band. A lot of great players played in that band. We used to play in the park – with dancers with no clothes on. It was wonderful. It was San Francisco. Hippies. The music is talked about sometimes in an over-isolatedly focused fashion. It's not often talked about as something produced by an entire environment or a set of cultural developments that happened to be synchronistically creating this cultural phenomenon.

I lived near Haight-Ashbury, up on Buena Vista East, and went to Keystone Korner, then a blues bar, to get a gig. It was next to the Keystone cops. [Keystone Korner was across an alley from the North Beach Police Station.] The owner of that blues bar, Freddie Herrera, who later opened Keystone Berkeley and Keystone Palo Alto, told me, "I hate jazz. It doesn't sell. I don't like jazz. But maybe you can buy the club and hire your own band and then you can, you know, have a jazz club." He was going to close it down; he was just going to sell it to the highest bidder. But I came along and he said, "Well, you can continue the club, but it's too small for what I want to do, and I need capital. I got this other room opening any day now, and I need to get the other place open and this place closed and let's get going here." So I came by a couple of days later with all the money I had in the world, which was about $8,000, and I put $5,000 down, and I financed the rest of the club. He had the banker there and I signed a note for another $7,500, and I paid $400 a month for a couple of years. That's how Keystone Korner started.

Freddie Herrera gave me a couple of nights for free before I officially opened as a jazz club. I had Jerry Garcia and Merl Saunders there and they were playing very psychedelic music. I didn't have to do anything but keep their names up on the marquee. I didn't even have to pay the band; I just had to get the place open. It was a transitional gig to help me get off the ground. We were repainting, getting the joint fixed up.

So they came in, and Jerry Garcia started to warm up in my office. He had one guy with him, an employee, who did nothing but roll joints. He was rolling joints, Jerry was playing, loud – ten on his amp – and I said, "No, this is not what I want to do." That really reinforced my wanting to make it a jazz club only. So that's what I did. We opened a jazz club, and eleven years later we closed down. But it was definitely a very wonderful ride. [Long pause] A rollercoaster ride.

I opened with the Michael White Quartet on June 7, 1972: Michael White, Kenneth Nash, Ed Kelley, and Ray Drummond. Two nights. Then Bobby Hutcherson's band came in and played for a couple of nights, and then McCoy Tyner played for a whole week. That's how we started.

Keystone Korner was definitely a bright moment in song. It was very much a cooperative effort, a very rare oasis where everybody seemed to be focused, with the same feelings about the music, and that's part of what made it a special experience. It was not only the care that I took of the musicians but the care they received from everybody working there.

There was Flicka [McGurrin, a waitress], who became quite a mover and shaker at Pier 23, but Keystone was her launching pad. Helen Highwater [Helen Wray, a waitress] – that's what I called her. You know, come hell or high water? That was my nickname for her. [Shouts] Helen Highwater! We loved her; we still do. Kristen [artist Kristen Wetterhahn] was working there as a waitress. Jack [San Francisco Poet Laureate Jack Hirschman] was handing out poems.

I had a series of managers. Tim Rosenkrans was there a long time. He was a bartender, an assistant manager, then manager; later on, he was one of the first managers of the Blue Note in New York. And then he died tragically at a relatively early age. Unknown reason. The main managers were Mark Dolezal, Tim Rosenkrans, and Nancy Swingle. Dolezal had long hair. He was a hippie-dippy. Great guy. The list of employees in [the notes for Dexter Gordon's CD series] *Nights at the Keystone* is the most comprehensive list, but there is no real recorded history of the Keystone. I mean, there isn't any accurate book, you know?

Claudia Deal, she was there a long time. She was a door person and a receptionist. A ticket booth operator. That was a very important position. The ticket booth was right out in front 'cause we sold tickets right on the street. Bob, he was there for quite a while.

Everybody that was working – whether it was the sound personnel (Milton Jeffries or Jim McKean or Mark Romero) or door personnel, the people working behind the bar, Mike in the kitchen, the managers and the assistant managers, and the waitresses and the waiters – everybody who was working there had the same kind of involvement with the music where they really, really got it and were able to really help support the music and to be responsive to the music.

For us at Keystone Korner, the greatest triumph in the world was paying the rent. And the phone bill. If we did that, we were supremely successful and happened to present the greatest music we could at the same time. But we never got any grants-in-aid or real solid support from anybody except a little bit of money from Bill Cosby and a few benefit concerts we did, especially in the early years.

In 1973 and 1975 we did some benefit concerts, which helped raise money for Keystone Korner. We had a benefit in 1973 with Rahsaan Roland Kirk, Freddie Hubbard, McCoy Tyner, Ron Carter, and Elvin Jones playing with the Black Classical Music Society, which is a concept I developed. We played at the Oakland Paramount Theater in February 1973 and we were able to raise enough money to buy a liquor license. And Rahsaan was a main motivator in actually having the idea to do that concert: "So let's get the guys together to do a concert, and we'll raise the money and we'll get a liquor license." And then we had another concert, early in 1975, and we were able to raise enough at the same Paramount Theater in Oakland to build a kitchen. And the kitchen enabled us to admit minors and make it a family club for the next eight years. But those things would not have happened without the musicians who donated their services to play. They didn't get paid anything. They just got their hotel and airfare, per diem expenses, but they worked for free.

I've never even heard of anything like that in the history of jazz – a bunch of musicians getting together and buying a club a liquor license. And then Grover Washington and George Benson getting together and deciding to do a benefit for us to buy a kitchen so that we could stay open and help the music out. Grover Washington Jr. was the best man at my wedding.

That's all part of the Keystone story. It's a place that struggled, but its struggle was also a part of why it was special. We didn't have any pretentiousness; there was no room for any hauteur or arrogance or remoteness or, you know, impersonality. We were so close to the street and so down with the people because we had to be. That's where we were. We were right on the street. So we had to make it right there on the street, and we had a network of people.

Our primary form of advertising was a network of volunteers who passed out flyers. That was the main way that we promoted Keystone Korner: with sweat equity. Nobody ever did a press release but me in eleven years 'cause I couldn't afford to hire a publicist. I would print them myself, then I would get some people to help me stuff envelopes and send them out. Here [in New York at the club Dizzy's], we have a publicity department, a promotion department, and all that, but in that era we just did it all ourselves. You know, I enjoyed it 'cause I could get creative with it – put little pictures and all.

I think I was extremely naïve in how low I made the ticket prices, and how I almost gave the music away for many years. My brother made a crack that was published in *Billboard* that one of my great, brilliant business moves was to buy the music retail and sell it wholesale. He said that in the pages of *Billboard* magazine, which did not make me happy, but there was a kernel of truth to that. My bank account regrets it, but I don't necessarily regret it. Cannonball Adderley was playing there, and I was charging $3 during the week and $3.50 on the weekend. For Cannonball Adderley. In 1973. I could have charged a little more than that. But I really wanted to make it affordable and I was quite a bit of a hippie in that regard. I was a psychedelic flower child in many ways.

Countless records were made there: Rahsaan Roland Kirk's *Bright Moments*; McCoy Tyner's *Atlantis*; Tete Montoliu, *Live at the Keystone Korner*; Dexter Gordon, *Nights at the Keystone*, which was just reissued [as a three-CD set] on Mosaic; Bill Evans, sixteen CDs, eight of which are called *Consecration* and eight of which are called *The Last Waltz*; Art Blakey, *In This Korner*, *Straight Ahead*, and *Keystone 3* – and two out of three of those records have early Wynton Marsalis on them. Red Garland's *I Left My Heart* is an important recording. There are numerous live recordings. *All the Way Live*, the only recording of Jimmy Smith and Eddie Harris together, was done there.

Some were made by us doing board tapes and then going to the record companies later on. Dexter Gordon's were tapes that Dexter and I made ourselves, and then when the time was right I asked Dexter about it, he liked the idea, and I went to Bruce Lundval at Blue Note. We put them out at a time when Dexter wasn't really doing very much, so it was very helpful to everybody concerned. Those are classic recordings.

Freddie Hubbard's were done by record companies, although one was a board tape that we were able to put out later. Freddie Hubbard was very well paid for that. We never made a dime on those. We never got paid for any of those recordings. In fact, I was so idealistic I never even charged the record companies. No, we didn't make money. We got no advances and no royalties for any of those recordings.

I was able to make a little bit of money from the Bill Evans recordings for the producer fees, although I didn't get any royalties. I've never gotten any royalties for any Keystone records, but I've gotten some producer fees for the work, a few thousand dollars for producing. All the hundreds of hours that you have to put into producing records.

. . . And there'll be more Keystone records as time goes on. There are thousands of tapes. But everybody has to get paid. It has to go through a very legitimate process for a record to come out [today]. There've never been any bootleg records I know of.

We definitely felt a really strong mandate to present a wide spectrum of music, and education was part of what we did. That was definitely intentional, but it was also part of our hippie-esque, utopian vision. And I think it was a good part. We definitely felt that the music, the whole spectrum of jazz music, went all the way from Jelly Roll Morton to Cecil Taylor, with everything in between. That was part of black classical music. That was part of improvisational, creative music. And that's how I feel to this day.

I was in San Francisco from 1967 until 1983. I moved to New York in 1983 and I've lived in New York ever since. My desire to leave San Francisco was accelerated by the change I felt in San Francisco itself, which at a certain point became much more yuppified, buppified, guppified. In the Reagan era of the early '80s, I felt San Francisco had totally changed. It wasn't the hippie paradise that I had enjoyed at the end of the '60s; it was about as diametrically opposed from that as I could imagine. So I got discouraged and felt the need to change venues, change partners and dance. I felt the desire at that time to come back to New York and continue my work. In certain ways, I had to come back here and start my life all over again, but that's just what I felt the call to do.

In retrospect, I have mixed feelings about that. I've been able to continue my work here and become a lot more involved in record production and work in New York City, which is, I think, the central home for jazz in the United States. It's not the end-all and be-all of jazz. I think jazz has become more broadly based than it was twenty, forty, fifty years ago. But at the same time, it's still jazz central, or one of the jazz central spots in the world.

I think the Keystone Korner was historically important in its ability to carry the banner during a very difficult time in New York [and other essential jazz locales]. [The jazz scene in] New York was not exactly flying high in the '70s. It was a very difficult era. There were musicians' union problems and there were discussions going on about cabaret fees, and all kinds of urban crises were going down in New York. They culminated in the '80s with the great crime waves and all kinds of things. But in San Francisco, even though rock and roll was ascendant coming out of the '60s and the whole culture was changing, Keystone Korner managed to be a real beacon for a full spectrum of jazz presentations in that era. It had its historical role to fulfill. It had a mandate to do something, and I think we were able to do it.

I can only imagine what we could have done if I had been able to hang in there in San Francisco and somehow keep Keystone Korner open, 'cause it would now be thirty-five years old. And that would be something to behold.

It was ironic. The club had already closed, I was here in New York City, and an article appeared in *USA Today* on the front page of the entertainment section about the three best jazz clubs in America. And there was my picture on the front page of the entertainment section of *USA Today* – after Keystone had closed.

Todd Barkan, Tootie Heath, 1977

Todd Barkan, Monty Alexander, 1977

Pharoah Sanders, Milton Jeffries, 1978

I guess it was his [Todd Barkan's]
booking and his relationship with
musicians that made it happen. But it
was the rest of us that made it work.
Helen Wray

Flicka McGurrin

I was working at Caesar's Latin Palace, the Latin club that Cesar Ascar-
runz owned. I had started there as a cocktail waitress, but it was way
out in the Mission and it was dangerous, and I was a single parent with
children. I just needed a job that was no responsibility, which was quick
cash, which was why I was cocktail waitressing. And so I realized that,
since jazz was my first love, it made more sense to work at Keystone
Korner because I lived right up the street.

So I went one night and asked for a job, and Todd's partner, whose
name escapes me, interviewed me out in the street and literally hired
me on the spot. Bald guy – remember him? And so I thought, "Well,
perfect. Now I'm working in one of my favorite places." I loved working there.

Helen Wray

I came over here [from Australia] in 1976 for a skiing vacation with a
suitcase and a pair of skis, and I'm still here. I went back to visit, but one
thing led to another and I just stayed.

I was twenty-five and green as grass, as Milton used to say. Pretty
naïve. I think I went to the Keystone the first month I was here, and
Bobby Hutcherson, George [Cables], Rufus [Reid], and Eddie [Mar-
shall] were playing. We'd heard about Keystone Korner in Australia.
People would come over here [to the States] and that's where you went
on the West Coast. It just had everybody.

My girlfriend and I were living on a boat down at the marina. A
friend we had met in Australia let us stay on it. Before I knew it, my
Australian friend had us enrolled in a classical music school in Pacific
Heights. (She's a classical pianist; I play amateur flute. I just do it because I like to play Bach for the fun of it.) The Music and Art Institute

on Jackson Street used to be the Japanese embassy. It had accommodations for about four students so we had this incredible attic room for about $30 each. We weren't working, we were students, so we were starving in Pacific Heights in this room with these views of the bay and watching *La Bohème* on TV and bawling our eyes out 'cause we could identify with it. We had this fire escape outside our room and we used to go out at night and go to Keystone and creep back in at three in the morning and have to be in theory class, which was right underneath our room, at nine. We were always late.

As students, we weren't really supposed to work, but there was this little club that opened downtown called Cristo's, owned by a Greek guy who had jumped ship many years ago; someone had given him a chance, and he built this business. I think I got $25 a night to be hostess in the jazz club, seat people. That's when I started getting to meet some of the musicians. At some point, it closed and I went to Keystone and asked for a job, so they put me in the ticket booth for a few months and then I started waitressing. Tim Rosenkrans was the manager at the time. I was working there a little while before I met Todd.

I must have been there about three years – 'til the very last night [of the club's existence]. I did the classical [music] thing during the day, then worked at Keystone at night, and even when I didn't work I'd go in if there was someone I wanted to hear.

Flicka McGurrin

Jim Polk was a doctor and one of the owners, or investors, at Keystone Korner. He would sit at the door a lot. He was there when Bill Evans played there. That was when Bill Evans's hands just looked so extraordinary I couldn't even believe that he was able to play the piano. His hands were like if you pour water into a rubber glove and make a water balloon, and you have all the fingers sticking out; that is what his hands looked like. And Jim Polk said that, unless he went into the hospital right then, he would be dead in two weeks. And he wouldn't go into the hospital. And he was dead in two weeks.

Stuart Kremsky

I was a soundman at Keystone. I started in May '78 and I was hired by the night manager, a man named Mark Dolezal. I remember hanging out outside, during a sound check for the Oliver Lake Trio with Michael Gregory Jackson and Pheeroan akLaff, and I just happened to meet Mark. We hit it off and became friendly and as near as I can recall, that was literally it. I did not have a lot of sound experience, but some. I don't remember applying or anything. We hit it off, and it was like, "Hey, can you do this?" "Oh yeah, sure." "You're hired." "Okay."

The regular soundman, a guy named Rich McKean, who has passed away, got really mad because he had no involvement in me being hired. So he disappeared – took off. Because I was the only soundman around, I was immediately pressed into service and worked for an entire week with the Red Garland Trio. Rich came back that weekend and managed to calm down, and I never worked another [full] week at Keystone.

I became the Monday night jam session guy, the Monday night soundman: set up the mikes, run a tape or not, depending on what Todd would say, and just keep things together. It was a relatively simple job in a lot of respects because you didn't have a lot of equipment to work with. It was all pretty basic. You didn't mike the drums because the room didn't need 'em. Basically, we miked the piano and bass and got the levels so everybody could hear. It was pretty easy.

Since I was only working one day a week, it really wasn't exactly a living, but it was a really cool place to be, a really cool thing to do, so I kept doing it. But you never made any money. I think a lot of people worked there 'cause it was cool – not because they loved working there but because they loved being there – and the easiest way to be there was to get a little work.

Helen Wray

Mike ran the kitchen. It was Middle Eastern falafel, greasy but good. Falafel and salads – it suited the place. Ora wasn't running the kitchen during the last few years of the club when I was working there, but she would float in. You always knew when she was in the club because she had this very distinctive perfume.

Everyone among the bartenders and waitresses had their own backgrounds and stories and how they got to Keystone. A lot of people with their own personalities. Emerson was a singer, a Buddhist, traveled a lot around the world, lived in various countries, had a very colorful life. Flicka McGurrin has done a lot of different things in her life. Kristen Wetterhahn, an extremely talented woodblock artist and activist, and socially conscious, was a lovely spirit. And then there was a beautiful, beautiful black waitress, Beverly Daniels, who's now a [California] Supreme Court judge in Alameda County. Tootie Bouchard, a North Beach character for many years. Gator, of course. We all loved Gator.

Gator was one of the bartenders and a beautiful spirit. He had sickle cell and he'd often have to take time out to be in hospital. I think Keystone was one of those places that kept him going. It was a labor of love to be there if you loved the music. With all those different personalities and backgrounds, it was like a family. And any time today when I run into them, it's just this lovely warm feeling.

Jack Hirschman

I was living with the artist Kristen Wetterhahn, and she got a job at Keystone [in 1977] as a waitress, and this became something a little more [personally significant]. Kristen was writing poems when we first met and made a whole book of poetry in a very beautiful, sibilant, cascading-on-the-page style. And then she became involved with her true love, which was visual art – graphic art – and she became really involved with the world of jazz. Kristen did an enormous amount of napkin drawings of jazz musicians and then she did an extraordinary woodblock of Cecil Taylor after he came to Keystone. I think it was one of the best things that she did. It was very treasured, and many people bought prints of it. And she's the only one who did a woodblock of Marilyn Monroe. If you pick up a book on Marilyn Monroe, you'll never see a woodblock. She did a wonderful one of Sonny Stitt. Jazz musicians became a big part of her life. And it was basically through Keystone.

Helen Wray

We were all treated like family – the people we worked with, the bartenders, most of the managers. Todd kind of came and went here and there, although he was always there to introduce the band and take care of things afterward.

Before working at the Keystone, I would go in there on my own. I was in my mid-twenties and the doormen would say, "Now, you be careful going home." Bob Johnson [one of the doormen] looked after all of us and various people who came in. He was such an imposing figure. These heavy-looking black doormen that everyone was scared of were the kindest, sweetest people. I don't think I've ever worked in a place like that. Everyone looked out for each other.

Dave Liebman

Every time you came, the crew was the same, which is always very comforting. That's the thing now about clubs; we have a different soundman every night. You don't even have a chance to say hello to anybody.

Todd had a guy at the door named Walid. With Walid at the door, it was great 'cause there was a feeling of security. You knew these cats and everyone was cool. . . . I always felt protected having those cats at the door.

Eddie Marshall

I was born in Springfield, Mass., but I moved to New York when I was a teenager. Actually I came here [to San Francisco] with a group called the Fourth Way. I was going to go back to New York because I figured there wasn't really all that much happening here after the Fourth Way broke up – for me, anyhow. And then Todd said he was going to open up this club.

I was working with Bobby [Hutcherson] a lot then. Todd contacted Bobby's rhythm section – James Leary, George Cables, and myself – and said, "You know, I'm going to open this club, man, and I'm going to need a trio." He was just going to bring [individual] people out 'cause he couldn't afford to bring whole bands out at first. And I was going to go back to New York, but these same people that I would be working with back there were coming out here. And I had a house I had bought in Oakland. And so I said, "Yeah, let's do it."

Helen Wray

George [Cables] was in the band with Bobby Hutcherson the very first night I went to Keystone. That was a couple of years before I started working there. I didn't really get to talk with him until I started working there. He was a very soft-spoken, sweet person. At that time he was almost the house pianist. He was living in Los Angeles, but he'd come up and play, say, with Leon Thomas, and then Todd would say, "Well, what are you doing next week? We have so-and-so coming." If they couldn't afford to bring a whole band from New York, then Eddie Marshall and George and sometimes James Leary would be the house trio. So they played with a lot of people that came in.

George Cables

I was living in L.A. but I was up in the Bay Area and at Keystone so much I think a lot of people started to think I was living in the Bay Area. When I was playing with someone [at Keystone], at the end or near the end of the week, Todd would say, "Hey, George – what are you doing next week?" I'd say, "Well, gee, I don't know. I think I'm off. I'm just going home." He'd say, "You want a gig? I got a gig for you." So I wound up playing with many more people: Toots Thielemans, Sonny Rollins, Art Pepper, Freddie Hubbard, Bobby Hutcherson, Dexter Gordon. Shoot. [Sings a passage from "Moody's Mood for Love" to remember the artist] "Ya smile and you're wrapped up in the magic, the music all around me." Eddie Jefferson, Richie Cole, Larry Coryell. There's so many people I worked with there, it's hard to name them all.

Helen Wray

I loved Milton – Milton Jeffries, the soundman at Keystone. They had a few different people over the years, but he was doing the sound the last few years. He was close to the musicians. He also recorded a lot of the concerts. He was like this big teddy bear, kind of like a brother figure to me. He looked out for you there, like Bob Johnson. You'd go up and visit him in the sound booth and have a smoke. He was another one of those people I met there that became family.

Stuart Kremsky

Milton was a really quiet cat. We didn't talk much; we didn't really get along very well, and I'm not really sure why. He was really quiet, and he was a little cranky at times, and I was kind of cranky too, so we didn't really hit it off very well.

Milton took a completely minimalist approach to sound. He would put up the mikes and do as little as possible. Sometimes, I think, he put up the mikes and didn't even turn them on. He'd never put them up very much, but the guys onstage felt better having mikes. He became the soundman after Rich left. And then he went on to work as the sound guy at Kimball's, where he did the same kind of thing – just putting up mikes and setting levels and leaving it alone pretty much – which was perfectly fine. These days, you get a lot of people who have more of a rock background; everything needs to be amplified and in your face, and they don't necessarily know what instruments sound like. They know what *amplified* instruments sound like. But Milton was old school. He was like, "We don't need amplification; we need reinforcement." That was kind of the vibe. Because when the drums are really hittin', you can't really hear the piano; you just want a little piano [amplification] so you can actually hear it. You don't want everything in your face.

His minimalist attitude fit his quietness, and the musicians really, really liked him 'cause he was so quiet and smooth. If there was any kind of hassle, it would dissipate because he was calm about it. And that's a really valuable thing in this kind of deal where you got people coming in late, and they got to do a sound check, and they're all hassled. He was really good at calming things down in case things got out of hand. That was his vibe.

Eddie Marshall, James Leary, 1978

Rahsaan Roland Kirk, 1977

Dexter Gordon, 1981

Betty Carter,
1976

Joe Daley, Sam Rivers, Anthony Braxton, Dave Holland, 1978

3

If you came to San Francisco, there was nowhere else to go. And the amazing thing, the paradox of the whole thing, is that the club and what went on in that club [existed] next door to a police station. This, of course, is big. This should be on page 1: "The Keystone Korner opposite the Keystone Kops." *Dave Liebman*

George Cables

God, the music was fantastic. I loved playing there because I could hear. The sound was great, the vibe was great, the music was live. Some rooms you play and you hear the note: *pssssst*. It sort of disappears or just comes to a thud, *boomp*, and that's it. But in Keystone, it was live; the sound reverberated, and you could hear the piano.

David Williams

Next to the Village Vanguard in New York, Keystone Korner was one of my favorite or maybe *the* favorite room for sound, for the bass. I like to hear it a certain way. And some rooms just have no personality. I'll spend all night fiddling with the amplifier. Some rooms make the bass sound out of tune. It would be in tune but the intonation would be off, and I'd be all night trying to tune the bass. So much of what we do is about the sound. It's all about the sound.

Carl Burnett

Keystone felt like a place where you could go and bare your heart. No matter what that was, you could stretch to whatever degree you could because the atmosphere was accepting. [Todd] brought the music in and stayed out of the way.

Flicka McGurrin

In Todd's place, there were long skinny tables. They were two-by-eights on restaurant stands and then they had the chairs behind them. Two aisles. Three sections for the three waitresses. It was usually Helen, Kristen, and me. And there was Roslyn. But basically I remember Helen, Kristen, and me as being sort of mainstays.

They had, I'd say, ten to twelve rows in front of Milton's sound place, that was up above. If you got in next to the wall, you were stuck; forget going to the bathroom. There was an aisle. In the center part were the rows in front of the bar, maybe ten across and eight rows [deep]. Then there was another aisle. And then there was another set of seats and those tables – two-by-eights – and then there was the wall that we had the art shows on. On the side, let's say there's maybe thirty [seats]. See, they really crammed them in. Probably close to two hundred. I don't know how he did it. And those little crummy bathrooms! You gotta hand it to him.

Terri Hinte

I remember Keystone not being a very comfortable place. One night I was there with Orrin and Lucy [Keepnews], and I just moved my arm to take off my jacket and in the process knocked over a raft of drinks behind me. [Laughs] So it was even tighter than I thought. And then, of course, the ladies room was not so great. It was right next to the stage, basically. The plumbing was not really very reliable. I guess that's the hippie/country part of it.

Todd Barkan

Keystone Korner, if you recall, had psychedelic murals all over the place behind the bandstand and then along one wall. The scarabs behind the bandstand were icons based on ancient Egyptian hoody-woody-boodie things, and then along the other wall, on your left, was Charlie Parker with angel wings, and all kinds of psychedelia – zodiac signs and all that. It was wild.

It was by a great lady, a great painter: Josie. She was a hippie and she used to come in, paint for a while, smoke a joint, paint a little more, go away. I never even asked her when she was coming back. She'd say, "When you gonna have a good week? I'll come and get some money." "Well, about two weeks from now, McCoy Tyner is going to be here." "Okay." And I'd give her a few hundred dollars. It took her about six months to do it. It appeared. [Barkan draws with his hands in a wave-like motion]

I couldn't pay Josie real well, but I paid her as well as I could, and she was very happy. We sold about 10,000 copies of that mural at a dollar each and she never even charged us a royalty. She got other large commissions based on that.

Orrin Keepnews

It was the kind of club where the sets might very well not start on time, for a variety of reasons. One might be that the owner was in the backroom talking to the musicians. He ran the place in a personalized way and he didn't seem to have any particularly well-established sense of business, or how you were supposed to operate to stay in business. What he did have was good jazz taste. He seldom brought in a bad act.

Maria Rosa Keys

It wasn't comfortable. It had those little narrow tables. The chairs were killers. It had those bent-cane chairs. But at that time, it didn't matter; it was totally fine. We'd park next door and walk down. I can remember it would get so hot in there sometimes that my hair would get totally flat and kinky. And then my whole cover was blown for whoever I was trying to flirt with.

devorah major

You could go to Keystone and not be hassled. And I also mean not be hassled as a woman. You know, a lot of times you go to places and you make sure you have a man in the group on the set because if you're real cute . . . I mean, this was the age when we weren't wearing bras, and it wasn't a political statement to us. We were young and didn't need them, you know what I mean? These older women were taking off their bras and burning their bras. That was not our trip. That was how the clothes looked best on us. But for guys, it was saying something about our sexuality or sensuality, and it meant free love. And so for black guys, it was making a statement that we were easier, which I didn't know at the time 'cause, as I said, I wasn't making a political statement. So it meant fending off people.

Keystone was a safe place to hear good music; I never thought of Keystone as a date place. I got dates to take me there, but that's because they'd say, "What do you want to do?" and you'd say, "I want to go to Keystone." But it was very much a place where you didn't have to have a guy to go. I can't remember going to the Both/And like that; I think I always went with a man. I'm not saying it wasn't a safe place. I'm just saying I didn't have that kind of relationship with it.

Helen Wray

I guess you'd call it funky. It was not very comfortable. You had long, narrow benches; people were very close together. It was hard to serve. You'd have these big heavy trays and the glasses were very heavy; they had these big mugs for Irish coffee. There was a lot of weight you were carrying, and when we had a full house, it was hard to maneuver. You had to pass the stuff down the rows and you had to be as conscious as you could and be as quiet as you could because you didn't want to distract from the music or the musicians. And it was as smoky as can be, so you had to be emptying ashtrays.

In retrospect, it seems hard, but at the time I was young, and the physical drawbacks of working there didn't seem to bother me. You were part of that experience for that night and it was exciting – who you were going to hear and what was going to happen, what new musical experience it was going to be from night to night.

Orrin Keepnews

Todd's place was a comfortable place, so therefore it lasted longer than sheer logic would have called for. The vibes from the place – I hate to be that corny – but it was both musician-friendly and audience-friendly. He doesn't take advantage of people; he doesn't give them a hard time when they come to work for him. It isn't, "Hey, did you know that the first set is supposed to have gone on five minutes ago?" Believe me, there are a lot of club owners who do that. He treats musicians like human beings, which sometimes means saying, "Hey, I'm not gonna be able to pay you 'til next week." But it [also means he didn't] get terribly uptight about enforcing all of the set times and such, didn't interfere in their problems, didn't say, "Gee, would you please play 'Happy Birthday' five minutes into the next set?" And he treats the audience like people. I mean, there are very well known, successful clubs, some still flourishing in New York, that are total cattle calls as far as the audience is concerned.

Calvin Keys

Keystone wasn't no million-dollar club. It was just a neighborhood joint that was made into a jazz room. [One could] smoke cigarettes and dope and everything else in there. But that was just part of that time in this country.

Carl Burnett

Some people came to hear the music because it was unique. It meant you were some kind of intellect – something other than a music lover.

The people who came [to Keystone] were music lovers. That made the difference.

devorah major	People in the Bay Area conceive of themselves as progressive, so going to Keystone was, in its own way, a hip act. You know, you're "hip" because you're going to the "hip" jazz club. But it would adjust you to what is right. You could come in with your little attitudes, but the music was so real that it would force you to get right.
Helen Wray	I think Keystone got a lot of the leftovers from the hippie-era audience. People were very casual. You know how, if you go to a club in New York, people will be older? We had a younger audience than we see in jazz clubs today. I think most people were there because they loved the music. Why else would they sit in such an uncomfortable room for a couple of hours, or wait for the second set for Dexter to show up?
Carl Burnett	It was comfortable. Comfort didn't depend on a particular thing; the comfort was *being* there. Comfort was the music and the time spent; everything that happened, you loved. That was the comfort. Even if you had to sit on the floor or stand up against the wall, it didn't matter. And then, if you had a chance to go back and talk with the band on top of that? Oh man!
Flicka McGurrin	People could do whatever they wanted in their seats 'cause nobody could see anything. The lighting in there was really, really dark. I always think clubs should be really dark. Lighting in clubs is so tricky and, as an owner, you can just lose it if the lighting is wrong. You know, your temperature goes right up.
	The most amusing part of cocktail waitressing was that you would remember people by the drinks that they drank. You might not remember their names, but you would remember them. If you saw them on the street the next day, you'd go, "Oh, Kahlúa and cream. Oh, Scotch and soda." So that was kind of the identifying factor. When you walked through the club to serve, you were always trying to get them to buy two, three, four drinks. So you were quick to remember.

The place wasn't full all the time, but when it was full for Dexter [Gordon] or for Art [Blakey and other headliners], trying to get in and get those drinks to people was really a feat. Those tables sort of tipped, and they all had ashtrays. People could smoke, which was so great. But it worked. Somehow, it worked.

Todd Barkan

We had ionizers coming from the ceiling, which took the smoke out of the air, and those ionizers also were designed to take the pot smoke out of the air, so that when you smoked a joint it didn't irritate people two rows up. It just went *psssht* – would disappear. And being right next to the police station, that was quite ironic that we could pull that off, but it was true. Nobody meant any harm; nobody was breaking the law. There was nothing, you know, "wrong." It was just all very positive energy there at Keystone Korner, next to the police station in San Francisco, in the psychedelic era.

George Cables

It didn't have a real bar, a service bar, but we didn't think about that too much. Bobby [Hutcherson] would go and get himself what he called a "dreamsicle" – orange and grenadine, or some other stuff. I think that was his concoction.

Stuart Kremsky

Typically, Keystone ran Tuesday to Sunday. Monday night was usually a jam session run by Tim, one of the day managers. Sometimes, if somebody was coming through town and they were only here on Monday, they'd book them on Monday. So I got to work with Toshiko Akiyoshi one night, and Woody Shaw one night. But mostly it was jam sessions and the occasional weekend poetry reading or something like that. I worked with Allen Ginsberg and William Burroughs one day. That was really cool. I was the special events guy.

I remember a lot of local cats playing 'cause it was an open jam. Jim Grantham, who's still around teaching, would play. I remember Bobby McFerrin playing on a Monday night, before anybody really knew who he was. There were some people that showed up every week and played.

Helen Wray

In general, I worked there three or four nights a week. It was $15 a night in cash, unless it was a really bad night; then, you mightn't get that and so you'd really depend on your tips. You weren't there for the money. We all loved working there. How many nights you ended up working depended on what the club was drawing and who was there. When the house was full, we'd have three waitresses on. If the second set was slower, one would go home. On nights that were very slow early in the week, you might only have one or two people on. Two bartenders when it was busy, one when [it was] not. One door person, and one person in the ticket booth.

I always liked working weeks with people like Dexter and Art because people tipped. And none of us wanted to work when Cecil Taylor was there because everyone came stoned and nobody tipped you anything – plus, you had to deal with Cecil and the band playing the whole set without a break. For me, it was very tense. But you know, everyone likes their own thing. He drew, but it was very subdued. It was funny, actually: the piano strings would break, and you weren't making any money.

Everyone did their own job and knew what had to be done. It's not like anyone had to tell anybody what they should do for the night. There weren't any problems that way or bad feelings. Now and then, there'd be some drama going on about something being turned off or not having enough money for this or that. The financial problems were the only problems; I don't remember personality problems or people not doing their part.

Stuart Kremsky

It was really informal in a lot of ways. The doormen were pretty strict, but it always felt like Todd's living room. Todd would come out and introduce the band, and everybody knew Todd. It was kind of like the only way he could [afford to] get these cats to play in his living room was to invite you in to pay.

Todd seemed to have a kind of hands-off attitude toward [soundmen] as near as I can recall. He trusted Rich [McKean] to take care of it, and Rich said who worked and when. There was a guy named Mark Romero who worked there for a while, and then Milton.

Eddie Marshall

There were some legal recordings that they did [subtitled] "Live at the Keystone." Those are good recordings. But there's one that came out with Cleanhead Vinson [*Redux*], another one he put out with Art Pepper [*San Francisco Samba*] – they were just from Milton's cassettes. Can you imagine that? They came out pretty good too. And Milton had a thousand cassettes.

Probably everybody knew that Milton was always taping. But they're really sad quality when you listen to them. They were just awful. You couldn't hear half the instruments, but I guess now you can. The one that he put out with Eddie "Cleanhead" Vinson has great sound – digitized, but it's great. A lot of cats got mad at Todd because some of those things came out and nobody really got any money, or else got paid later, and I said, "You think you're gonna make a million dollars off o' some record that Todd puts out of Cleanhead Vinson?"

Stuart Kremsky

Virtually everything that was played at Keystone Korner was recorded either on cassettes or on small reels of tape. Those tapes over the years have traveled around the country. A certain quantity of them right now are living in this vault [at Fantasy Records]. Todd Barkan sent them here for safe keeping.

I think there's only about seventy or eighty reels, and maybe two hundred or so CDs – I've never really counted. Some of the CDs actually are of the tapes – a number of things were recorded directly to cassette – but we don't have any cassettes here.

Al Young

I enjoyed going there to hear music because it was like going to a living room. It was small enough that you could see just about everybody in the place at any given time, and I would usually sit in front over by the piano, sideways, so I could look at the stage and look at the audience. It was an experience for me not only in listening to music, but a sort of jazz sociology – just observing behavior, watching how people reacted or interacted with the music.

I've never forgotten the night that I was sitting at an angle where I could see this young woman from Europe who was watching Bobby Hutcherson play. She was absolutely mesmerized. He was on the stage and she was at the table closest to the stage, right up under him. And I actually watched her go into a kind of trance under the influence of his music and his behavior. And he observed her, saw what was happening, and, at a certain point, I could tell that he was playing to her. He hit something and she just went completely out. I couldn't tell if she was stoned, or what was happening there. But you could see such things in Keystone. There was an intimacy, absolutely.

Stuart Kremsky

Thursday night was usually considered by the insiders to be the night for the music. Friday and Saturday nights were the big nights for crowds. Tuesday night, people [musicians] would open and get used to the room; Wednesday, they'd be a little more used to the room and more relaxed 'cause they wouldn't be traveling. And by Thursday night, everybody was totally into it. The cats would have more of a chance to rehearse in the afternoon and they'd really get a feel for the room. Friday and Saturday nights would be really crowded, and Sunday night it would be, "Okay, we're outta here!" But Thursday night was the night if you really cared about the music.

People don't tour like that any more. There aren't nearly as many working bands. It's different.

Dave Liebman

The main thing that is important to Todd is that you're hittin'; you're for real; it's immediate. It's not about the style – style is a matter of taste – but the sincerity and validity and the seriousness with which someone verses themselves in the music. That's what he was about. He loved that. You'd get off the stage and he'd say, "You're hittin'. You're hittin'."

Jaki Byard, 1978

Liberation Music Orchestra, 1979

Joachim Kuhn, Toots Thielemans, 1977

George Cables, Eddie Marshall, 1977

Lester Bowie, 1977

Don Cherry, Ayisha Knight, Cathy Brownlee, 1978

Two young cute black women . . . you can go backstage at any jazz concert you want.

devorah major

Eddie Marshall

The backroom. A glorious room. That couch was one of the most comfortable couches in any room, I'll tell you. And if they wanted DNA evidence about anything, they could probably get it right on that couch. [Laughs] It's funny, I look at that couch and I can see Flora [Purim]'s little girl sleeping on there, my kids sleeping on that couch in the back, and yeah, little Ayisha. Oh man. You could call it a family-oriented place – [Laughing] – even with all the carrying on.

Most backrooms were small rooms. Like the Five Spot. I don't know – did the Five Spot even have one? Birdland had a pretty nice one, but it was still small.

I really love Yoshi's. I find it a very musician-friendly place. You know, they have a backroom and everything, but it could be anywhere. Either you can't get back there, or when you get back there, it's really small, very cold. They don't have people's autographs on the wall.

Dave Liebman

Todd was very generous. If you had to sleep, you could sleep in the back; you could sleep all night in the back in the office there.

Helen Wray

The backroom was where musicians hung out after the concert. It was between the main room and Todd's office. And it was covered in incredible photographs of everybody who played there. You'd go back and talk to people, catch up with them. It was like the private part of the club.

David Williams

As many times as I worked at Keystone Korner over the years, a lot of my time was spent gazing at the walls back there by the old couch – pictures on the ceiling, on the walls – and each time I'd be amazed to discover the stuff, even though it was the same old pictures. But there was something about the walls. I'd just walk around in a daze, looking at the walls in the backroom.

Dave Liebman

Serious young guys who are in the music always want as much as possible a touch with the past. People in the backroom were talking stories; musicians are always talking stories about so-and-so, or when he played that, or when he played with him, whatever. So in a way, for a young musician, which I was, to go in the back and hear this stuff from my heroes was an education.

The backroom was a serious hang. You really hung and listened. Todd always had something to listen to: "Check this out. Check that out." Usually Dexter [Gordon] or Rahsaan [Roland Kirk]; he loved that stuff. Todd was a teacher in a way. He knew that music and he was informing you – someone like myself, or Richie Beirach, who I was with a lot – he was informing us of our lineage. You need that; you need guys who know it. A club owner's tastes set the vibe of a club. And Todd was basically conservative. He liked the older cats playing straight-ahead jazz. He was coming from the tradition, but he wasn't opposed to other things. My first band was half electric, half acoustic. We played Indian stuff. We did everything. It was fusion, and he was cool. He had avant-garde guys there. He was pretty open to that. But when he would get you in the back, he would invariably say, "Check this Dexter [recording]." He would put on one of the masters and say, "Dexter was here last week."

Calvin Keys

There was another door that went downstairs into the basement. That was strictly for the cats. He had some storage rooms down there, and the heaters. It wasn't dirt floors. It was in good shape. They had bathrooms down there. And if somebody wanted to have privacy, they could. The regulars, the carte blanchers, knew about the downstairs. That's where all the musicians hung out anyway. Very seldom did you see the wives or the girlfriends.

Laurie Antonioli

That backroom. I don't know if I was really bold or somehow I had been invited, but I remember going back and sitting on that couch and just watching and listening to everybody talk. There was no other place where you could meet that many great musicians at once. You might find people around and about, but the Keystone was like a magnet for everybody. I was so enchanted by every single thing that was going on – the good, the bad, and the ugly. I didn't realize how special it was, of course. None of us did.

And I feel like I definitely know things that people educated in universities and institutions are not going to get. Because it really wasn't about [the musicians] telling us how to play over a Lydian scale; it was more like what happened to you when you were on your way to the gig, and finding a funny way to tell the story. Just the level of humor, dark humor. Jazz humor.

Eddie Marshall

Oh man! We'd just be back there bullshittin'. Suppose Dexter came in. Dexter would have whole families that came to see Dexter. People that he knew would drive up from L.A. Same with all the acts. When Tito [Puente] would come, the Latino people would be there. It would be a gas. It was just a really, really warm and friendly place.

Helen Wray

And then there's the dealers. Besides everyone's friends and various musicians going back to talk to the band or whoever's back there – a constant flow of people coming and going – there were a few shady characters, the dealers. Most nights, someone would come in if the musicians wanted anything. It was part of that time. There was always someone to supply whoever needed it, depending on who was playing. They all did it. And the ones who are still alive stopped doing it. It was certainly part of what was going on there. I didn't really think about it too much.

devorah major

My friend Meg was a backroom kind of gal. I tended to be much more shy, and she'd say, "Let's go backstage and say how much we loved it. C'mon." We would just walk through the people and go backstage. She could just do it. We met Pharoah Sanders and hung out with him and one of his musicians afterward. He just wanted to go to bed with one of us. [In a little girl's voice:] "No, I like your music, that's all."

But the next day, he comped us, and we came in and sat down, and he came and gave me a kiss and said, "You are one classy gal." I was like,

"No, I'm not classy. I just don't know you and you don't turn me on."
I'm not a groupie. It's not my thing.

Carl Burnett

Initially, people didn't know or think that they could walk backstage and talk to the musicians. When they did it and nobody really stopped them, there was a feeling initially that everything was going to get out of hand, that they were going to charge the band. But everybody was sensible enough to recognize the fact that the musicians needed to rest after the music, so people were patient. A few people would come back [after] the first set, a few people came back [after] the second set, but they didn't abuse it. I think that had to do with their respect for the situation that had developed. Todd didn't interfere with it; that was the uniqueness of Keystone – everybody had to give. The people who came, they gave, and the musicians enjoyed it. So they always wanted to come back.

George Cables

I did like the fact that you could go in the backroom, that it was open. I mean, people would come in and hang. I could see them coming from the front door *zzzzzzoop* into the back! You could go and sit right there and talk to people and there was a couch just for that. I met a lot of people. I can remember talking with Esther Phillips, and she was telling stories left and right, nonstop. Stan Getz. If you weren't upstairs doing something, maybe you were downstairs in the basement, and you might see Woody Shaw. Boy, it was just great. I made a lot of friends at Keystone.

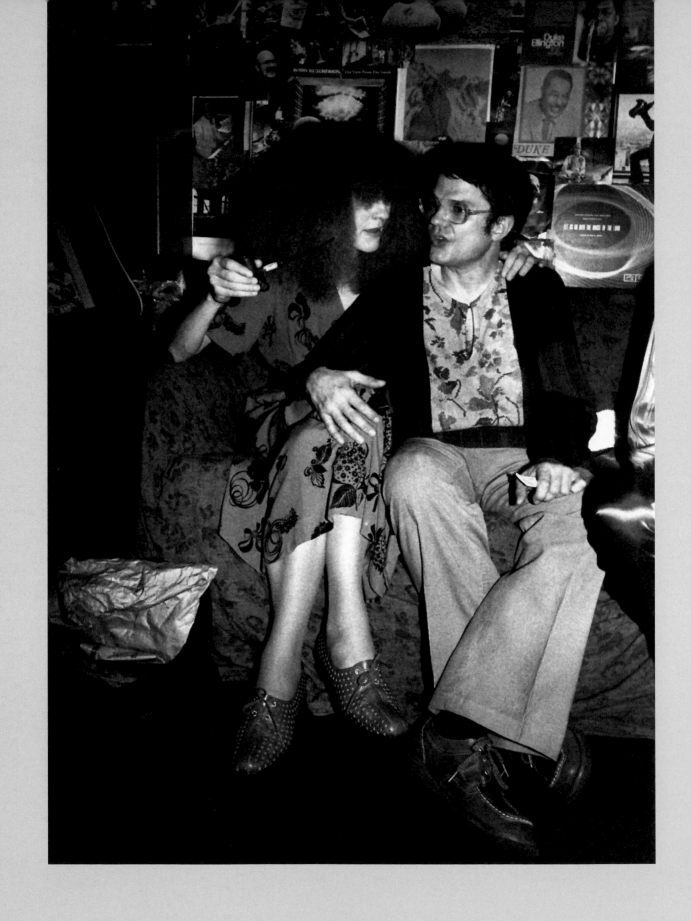

Carla Bley, Charlie Haden, 1978

John Heard, 1982

Ed Blackwell, Eddie Moore, 1978

Eddie Moore, Julian Priester, Merl Saunders, 1978

Sundance with Andre Marshall, 1977

[Rahsaan Roland Kirk] was not going to let me say no to making Todd a kitchen. So I did. I basically did it as a favor to Rahsaan.

Ora Harris

Ora Harris

I came to California from Boston where myself and a girlfriend had started an organization called the Black Avant Garde. '70, '71 – about like that. A minister allowed us to have the basement of his church on Friday nights and Saturday nights, and we made ourselves a jazz club. We put in tables and made tablecloths; we shopped and made food; and it was just absolutely wonderful. There were many, many good, talented musicians in Boston at the time: Bill Saxton, Ralph Penland, Justo Amario. Many, many – I can't name them all now. But we thought they were all so good that we started our little club. And it worked out well because the people just loved it. My girlfriend Mattie and I, we would make brown rice and chicken cacciatore, cornbread and fried chicken and cabbage. Good, basic soul food. We made banana nut bread and carrot cake and, of course, the word got out that there's not only music but there's really good food.

And you know, Boston was the home of the Jazz Workshop and Paul's Mall, so all of the name musicians would come from New York to the Jazz Workshop. Word got out that there were these two ladies that had this little organization called the Black Avant Garde in the basement of a church. Rahsaan Roland Kirk heard about us and wanted to come down because Rahsaan loved to eat, that was his thing. He also loved being out late at night. He had someone to bring him, and I fed him, and when he was finished eating, he was so happy he played. He almost played all night at our little place. Well then, the word got out that this was the place to come after work. People like Freddie Hubbard came down. A lot of name musicians would come down. I don't know if they came down to hang and play and jam or if they came to eat. But they were all there.

Ora Harris

53

And then I made the decision to move from Boston to San Francisco. I think I got here in '74. I'd been in San Francisco maybe seven or eight months, a little less than a year, and Rahsaan Roland Kirk was booked at the Keystone Korner. Rahsaan and I and his wife, Dorthaan, we had become close friends. He was thinking at one point that he would leave New Jersey and move to Boston, and I was helping the two of them look for housing in Boston, so we spent a lot of time together. So, of course, when he came to Keystone Korner I went to see him, 'cause now we're friends.

We went down, had a good time; he and I, we talked and carried on. Then, maybe a month later, I got a call from Rahsaan Roland Kirk to say, "I have a friend, his name is Todd Barkan, and he has a club, Keystone Korner – you know, the club that you came down to see me at."

"Sure."

"Well, he wants to have a liquor license and in order to have a liquor license he's going to need to sell food. He's going to have to have a kitchen and food in order to . . ."

I said, "Rahsaan, I really don't want to do food because I want to start back to school and I don't think that I can."

"Oh, you can do it for a little while. You don't have to do it for long. Just do it long enough that he satisfies all the needs to get his license."

I said, "But Rahsaan, I'm not a cook. I just cook for my family and my kids."

He said, "Oh yeah, you can cook. I've eaten your food from the Black Avant Garde. You can cook; it'll work." He just would not take no for an answer.

There was a real special relationship always between Todd Barkan and Rahsaan Roland Kirk. Todd absolutely loved Rahsaan. And, of course, Rahsaan just adored Todd. Rahsaan always liked to put his special people together. He had an art for that. He was not going to let me say no to making Todd a kitchen. So I did. I basically did it as a favor to Rahsaan.

There was no kitchen there at Keystone Korner; there was a closet between the backstage green room and the garage, basically. He brought me down to look at the room and I looked at this little hole in the wall and said, "Oh my, how can I make a kitchen?"

[But] I did. One Saturday morning, Todd Barkan and his father came by to pick me up. We went to a supply store and bought a stove range and a sink, a refrigerator and a huge chopping block, and I made a kitchen: Ora's Kitchen at Keystone Korner. And it started from there.

I was there from about '74 to '82 – somewhere like that. I was going to school in the evening. It was very difficult, going to school and doing those late nights at Keystone Korner, but it was so much fun.

Miles Davis came in to open Todd's new room for the kitchen opening. So I looked at it like, Ora Harris and Miles Davis open [at] Keystone Korner on the same date in 1975. And yes, we had a fight on the first day, Miles and I. It's funny now; it wasn't funny to me at the time. I was not a playgirl. I was just serious, you know. "I'll be your sister, I'll be your friend, I'll be your cousin. And that's it." That was very easy for all the musicians to get real soon. And when Miles Davis came in, he didn't want a cousin or a sister or anything like that. He just wanted to be touchy-feely. So we had a little fight about that.

I cooked basically the menu that I did at the Black Avant Garde because I knew it went well, and everybody who ate it loved it: brown rice, chicken cacciatore, cornbread, sautéed vegetables, fried chicken, banana bread, carrot cake, and Ora's special punch that everybody loved 'cause it was sweet. During that time, remember, people were trying very hard to keep up with their vegetarian diet. To come and have some brown rice and sautéed vegetables, cornbread, and Ora's punch was a real treat.

It became very special because I would come down in the evening early to start my preparation for dinner, so by the time the musicians would come in from the road to sound check, I'd have started my food preparation. When they came in the door of Keystone Korner, as opposed to smelling last night's beer on the floor, or the wine – you know, that club smell – they could smell vegetables and food. They would walk in and say, "Mmmm, what's going on here?" and then it was a problem getting them to the rehearsal stage because everybody wanted to have a little snack before they played.

That was always fun seeing the joy that it brought to them when they would find that there was really some serious food, but food that they knew, grew up with. Having cornbread when you came in for sound check, some real vegetables – you know, everyone loved it. I think Todd liked it because a lot of them, once they came in for sound check, would have a little bit to nibble and then would come back early and order their food to eat before they went on. So there was never any worry about anyone being late because they came in early to eat their food. I can't think of anyone that didn't want to come to work. And, of course, Todd was so happy and proud because he would look back there, see them eating, and they were happy – and on time.

Todd ate most of his meals there. He would walk by the kitchen and he would say – he called me "Lady Harris" – "Lady Harris, I'm ready to eat now." I would take his plate in the back of the office room, and he would sit there and eat. He loved chicken cacciatore. He loved Ora's punch, just a creation of stuff that was tasty: juices, fresh orange juice, some pineapple juice, [things] like that. Everyone who came and worked there would eat.

[I'd] send some plates up to the box office when they were taking the tickets. The waitresses would stand there at the counter and eat. My biggest flattery was when McCoy [Tyner] wanted me to make him a carrot cake to take home with him when he left. I made him a cake and a little carry box and wrapped it up, and he took it on the plane and went home.

It became the culture of the club with the musicians, the kitchen did. I had one of those half doors, where the bottom is closed and the top you would open and there was a little counter. So I was behind the counter in the kitchen, [and] the musicians coming from the little sitting area had to walk by the kitchen to go to and from anyplace. You name one – McCoy, Sonny Stitt, Dexter Gordon – they would all stop to order their food when they came off the stage. Then, they would order food to bring home to their hotels when they were ready to leave.

I can't tell you all the songs that were played to me at that window. Rahsaan Roland Kirk one night had his band coming out from the dressing room, the backroom, and singing with the band he made up a song about my chicken. On their way to the stage: "Eat that chicken, eat that chicken, eat that chicken, now." Rahsaan. Rahsaan Roland Kirk. It was pretty special. [Editor's note: Kirk was performing Charles Mingus's composition "Eat That Chicken."]

Art Blakey, he didn't eat a lot. I don't know why. But he always wanted rice and vegetables and a little piece of chicken.

It started off to be a concession, but we changed it a bit because I ended up paying my salary from it. Money was a difficult issue at Keystone Korner. I knew Todd was having many problems financially. Todd was very good and fair with me. Todd would many times pay for some of the food. He just allowed me to have the kitchen and I made very good money. There were a few times when I was able to help pay a few salaries to the band from cooking. I think the price was something like $2.50 for a dinner (that's my recollection – I could be a little off) and the menu for the food was very inexpensive. I think the fruit punch was maybe fifty cents. It was no money. But it would add up because Todd booked well. So many times, the place would be full, and most of the people would want to eat.

Around '76 or '77, Todd added a dinner evening where people would come in early and have dinner and then come to the show. Dinner was probably from 6:00 to 7:30 or 8:00. I thought it was very smart because it allowed him to bring in the local talent that was here in the Bay Area. People like James Leary would come in with a group; Katrina Krimsky, she was a pianist; a lot of people like that would come and play during the dinner hour. That would be maybe for a couple of hours, and then the music [by the headliner] would start at 8:00. People would come in early for dinner so therefore I was able to make money.

It was just a wonderful, wonderful place to be. It was so special for me 'cause I didn't deal with a lot of things like the drugs and all of that; it didn't come into my life so much there in the kitchen because I had such respect from all of the musicians as well as Todd. So I had an isolated island where they came for their eating needs, and if you come [and] someone feeds you, then you're happy.

Woody Shaw and Bobby Hutcherson and [George] Cables – I fed them all the time. Woody Shaw, we just adopted each other. I was his sister. Bobby and Woody would hang out at the kitchen, and when I would feed them, they would sing this song "Cherry Pie" 'cause they're happy now, they had some food, life looks good, the music's gonna be playing, and they would just break out in song. And of course I loved that.

Charles Lloyd was a very devout vegetarian. I mean, really serious. He had been on a fast for quite a long time, and one night he came to the kitchen after he finished the set and said, "I want to talk to you. Close the door." I closed the door to the kitchen. "Do you have any more of that pot likker from the sautéed vegetables?" I said, "Yeah." I'm thinking, "What does he want with that?" He took the pot and he drank that pot likker juice, and he was just so happy because he was not eating, but the nutrients from that juice – from the vegetables, which were cabbage and carrots and broccoli and greens, peppers and red peppers – gave him such energy. He was so happy; he was ready to play again.

Because I had relationships with so many musicians, and the kitchen, as you know, was so small, I had a rule that no one could come in the kitchen. That was just the rule. (Well, of course, Charles Lloyd came in to drink the juice from the vegetables.) But there was one person who insisted upon coming into the kitchen 'cause he wanted to be the only one to have been in the kitchen: Les McCann. So we had a really big fight. I couldn't let him break the rule. Musicians want to chat and talk; now, they're going to be in the tiny kitchen where I'm trying to cook, and that was a no-no.

So on Saturday, for his performance, he walks in with these two bags. He has a Bundt pan and all the fixings for a cake that he was going to cook that night with me. He brought his eggs, all of his ingredients, everything. And when he came in with all of his supplies, with all of my rules I [nevertheless] had to let him make the cake. Les McCann, he was such a character. He was determined to be in that kitchen. Made the cake, put it in the oven, and went onstage. He cut it up and shared it. It was good. He made a lemon cake.

I thought it was a wonderful culture at the time, regardless of a lot of the negatives that people talk about – the drugs and this and that. I think a lot of that was going on but again, remember now, I was naïve about a lot of things like that. I was just dealing with the excitement of these wonderful, wonderful musicians. My feeling was the waitresses were just overjoyed to be in that environment. The door people to the sound people to the waitresses, the waiters, everyone who worked there knew: "This is where I want to be." I didn't feel that way initially because I was doing a favor, I thought, for Rahsaan Roland Kirk. But then, as time passed, I became one of them. This is where I should be; this is where I want to be. It was like the pulse of the Bay Area. Todd had such love and admiration for the musicians and the most important thing to Todd was that everybody be happy. Most of all, the musicians must be happy.

Being across from the police station was pretty neat. Once I drove up – and there's not much parking there at the Keystone Korner – I'm driving in fast, I have to get the kitchen going, got to get the stove on, got to get my chicken on, and I'm rushing. I got all my food in the car, have nowhere to park, and I want to get there before the band comes in, get something smelling [good], and I have nowhere to park. "What am I going to do?" So I parked directly in the police station's parking lot, and I said, "Okay, I'm parked here. Now what am I going to do? You got to start cooking."

The spot that I parked in was the closest to my entry to the kitchen, which is right there in that little alley, where the police parked when they were on the run. So I go into the police station: "I'm Ora Harris. I'm the cook at the Keystone Korner. I'm in a jam. I need to park my car here. I gotta get my food out because I got to cook. If you let me do this, I promise you I'll bring you a carrot cake in about three hours."

"Okay." From that day on, I had a permanent parking spot. I just had to take them a carrot cake.

Jane Fonda at that time was married to [Tom] Hayden. They came down and hung out at Keystone Korner and had a great audience and spoke. It wasn't a fundraiser. They were looking for an audience, and trying to talk to people, to inform them about the [Vietnam] war – trying to get people involved and be knowledgeable of what was happening. I think that Tom was running for office as well. But it was very well done. And very, very well received. And, of course, I made little snacky-poos and made cakes and banana nut bread and was trying to impress Jane Fonda, whom I adored. I served her some fruit punch. She came in the kitchen and talked with me, ate some food. I was just in awe of it all.

Bill Cosby used to come down often for people like Dexter, or Sonny Stitt. Sonny Stitt was just a wonder. That was always a special treat when Sonny Stitt or people like that were there because they brought out all of the wonderful musicians from all over the Bay Area from the days of the Fillmore West era.

I would sometimes come from the back of the kitchen and just kind of peek out, and you could just see smiles. Now Todd is happy, 'cause he's pacing. He's walking from the front to the back because everyone is smiling, the room is full, money is flowing, and everyone's happy. So Todd is just pacing back and forth. Just smiling.

The musicians really played. They didn't care about getting off the stage; they didn't look at their watches; they didn't look at the clock to see if they played for forty-five minutes or two hours. They would just play, it would feel so good, and the audience would be screaming.

Everyone loved to play there. I can say for sure Betty Carter because I became her manager during the time she was there. I met Betty when I was in Boston doing shows there. When I got to Keystone Korner, I thought, "Well, we just have to have her here." She came in – I think it was around 1976 – and she just loved it. Then, of course, Todd brought her back all the time. I have a picture of Betty just before going onstage or coming off, having a good time, eating off a chicken leg – at the window there.

McCoy loved coming. Again, Todd and the people who worked there treated the musicians so well, with lots of respect. And I did the same in the kitchen. Everyone loved to play at the Keystone Korner. Pharoah Sanders and Yusef Lateef absolutely loved it. Cannonball Adderley would just have a ball. They always talked about how much they liked playing there and wanted to come back. That was the key to me.

If you go and play a room and want to come back and you haven't left yet, that is a true sign of your happiness.

Many of them would bring their wives with them to Keystone Korner because, after all, you are in San Francisco; you're in a club where you're getting lots and lots of respect. There were people that would bring the kids. The wife would come down for the first set and the kids would fall asleep. You know, it really had a nice little family vibe back in that backroom.

At that time, my son was just a young kid and I didn't make him listen to jazz or anything like that, but sometimes he had to come to work with me because I wanted to see him, know where he was. Therefore, now he loves jazz. He was raised around it. He knows who Miles Davis is and knows the music and has been teaching it to his son. He spent a lot of time at Keystone Korner listening to the music. People would sign recordings for him, make a fuss over him – you know, because all the musicians were very respectful.

It would be hard to create that today 'cause things have changed so much. I'm sure the economy has a lot to do with that. You need money, you want to hurry and get offstage, you don't want to tire yourself, you want to get on to the next date, and all of those things.

Periodically, I get to talk to people that were there during that time and you just mention Keystone Korner and an artist's name and faces just light up. There was nothing like it. I don't think there has ever been a club like Keystone Korner. It was the saddest day for San Francisco when Keystone Korner closed. And you know, we've never had a jazz club since in the city. Yoshi's is coming now to the city, but there'll never be another Keystone Korner. People talk of the days before, like the Blackhawk and the Both/And. Those were some wonderful, wonderful moments, and Keystone Korner came in from there. But after Keystone Korner, that's it.

Art Blakey, 1977

McCoy Tyner, 1977

Dewey Redman, 1978

Betty Carter, 1976

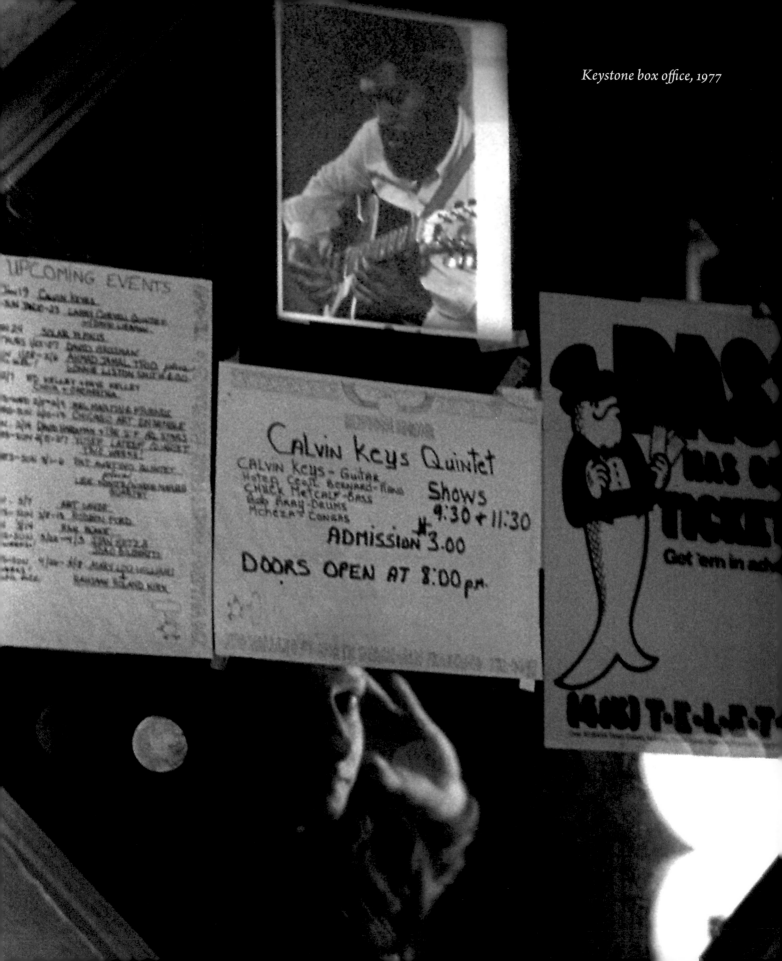

Keystone box office, 1977

I always got paid, so I have nothing to complain about.

Flicka McGurrin

Eddie Marshall

You never saw Todd riding around in a Cadillac [laughs] or doing anything but paying rent when he could make it.

Calvin Keys

He would take chances. He would hire musicians from back east, not knowing whether he was going to make any money with them but knowing that a lot of people out here wanted to see them. Where else did Art Blakey and the Jazz Messengers play in San Francisco? He must have made some kind of a living, but he didn't make a killing. I guess the big ones paid [for] the little ones.

Eddie Marshall

People came out here and they couldn't bring their own rhythm section. I mean, it really kills me when people say that Todd was such a shyster. A shyster from what? Hell, you know, even then, what it cost to bring somebody out here to play plus put them in a hotel? And knowing [Todd] was going to have to have some kind of benefit, or get money from his dad – or [have to face] the rent going up . . . ? He could never, never afford [all those rising costs]. There was no way, I'll tell you. He just did it anyhow. Those people that own that building, they kept raising the rent, and they wanted that to be a commercial venue, so he was always under fire.

Carl Burnett

I played there with Freddie [Hubbard] several times, with Eddie Harris a few times, and with Buddy Montgomery once, I think. I played there with Horace [Silver] a couple of times and once with Bobby [Hutcherson]. Todd put us up in some strange places but that never was an issue. As long as we were together and we were going to play, it didn't matter.

I was with Horace at the Sam Wong Hotel in Chinatown. I'd never stayed there before – or since. [Laughs] It was just like some of those hotels I stayed in in Japan when I first went. You go to use the bathroom and take a shower and everything in one spot. The beds were too short. The Sam Wong was rough, but in that situation you put up with anything. It didn't matter 'cause I was there to play music. That took precedence over everything else that was happening.

David Williams

We stayed at the Sam Wong about two or three blocks away on Broadway. And that should be a chapter in itself. I believe it was $11 a day for a single room. And it was an extra dollar for a TV and $2 for the color TV, which you could never get. Every time we'd go there, I'd ask Sam, or son of Sam [for a color TV, but] it was always out because they only had two. You could hear them coming down the hall with these carts on the squeaky wheels.

Once, I got the color TV. Man, I was in luck. I was signing in and he said, "Yes, we have the color TV." I paid him the $2, they brought it to the room and turned it on, and, man, it was the purplest color. [Long laughter] This was some stuff to make your eyes go bad. It was horrible. I took it back and told him to give me the black-and-white.

Sam Wong was a legendary hotel. I didn't even know they had a suite. I went up to Ornette [Coleman]'s room and he had the suite. I couldn't believe it. He had a little hotplate where he could cook. That was the suite.

Helen Wray

Those double bills had to have lost money. It was probably not financially a wise thing to do 'cause the club always struggled; it wasn't a profit-making business. Todd did try to give the musicians what they deserved. And sometimes we just didn't make it. It was a pity they couldn't have had a grant, or it wasn't better supported, because it was just the most extraordinary place for music. It was a musicians club.

Orrin Keepnews

He ran this club in what I clearly came to realize very soon was a most un-businesslike way, a most personalized way. He didn't pay much attention to the normal rules of behavior in a number of ways. For instance, I was always fascinated by the fact that, when I first started going there, he didn't have his liquor license straight. I mean, they were serving beer and wine, and they couldn't go any further, and he left it that way for a while. I thought this was something deliberate, perhaps. Maybe you don't want your customers getting too drunk too easily or whatnot. But then I discovered it was just that he hadn't bothered getting it taken care of. He didn't have a very well-organized commercial sense.

But when they did get a liquor license, a full-scale liquor license, then you became really aware of how hard it was to get served with any regularity in that club. He didn't get that liquor license so that he could get rich selling people drinks, which is a characteristic of jazz clubs. I don't know whether it's the people waiting on tables or standing still listening to the music or what, but it's always been my experience that it's very hard to get drunk in a jazz club. I can't necessarily analyze it for you, but it sure was true of Todd Barkan's club.

Stuart Kremsky

As a business proposition, it seemed to be a complete disaster. You bought liquor at retail. I was there in '78, and I imagine at one point he hadn't paid his liquor bill and got cut off by the wholesalers. So when you ran out of brandy, somebody had to go around the corner to the liquor store so you could pour drinks. You don't make any money on the door in the music business; you make money on liquor, and when you're buying liquor at retail, you're not making any money. So it was really tough.

Flicka McGurrin

He used to have to go buy the booze every night down at Coit Liquor. He'd come back with a big cart full of booze, which was totally illegal because when you have a club you have to buy the booze from the distributors. He couldn't afford to run the club the way it needed to be run. When you think about the amount of money that he spent to get those musicians out there – their plane tickets, their hotel rooms – that's a lot of money. I don't know how he did it. Well, he didn't do it, obviously, so that's not a big mystery. But that is really an enormous undertaking, and it's very difficult to make things happen.

Dave Liebman

Todd landed in the right place to do it. I don't think he could have done it as easily in Denver, Dallas, or L.A., to be sure. For whatever reason, he picked the right place to do a club and have the right ambiance. In that time, San Francisco was one of the good cities to be in – this and New Orleans are the only two cities besides New York with any kind of vibe. If you were in North Beach, besides the police, you had to deal with somebody. This was a closed shop. It's politics in a big city. You don't just walk in from Ohio and open a candy store – especially with liquor. Everybody said, "How'd he get away with it? He must have paid off . . ."

I said, "I don't believe he had any kind of money to pay off." They just looked the other way. It was San Francisco. It was North Beach. Lifestyle was understood. Cops didn't bother you. I am sure he had his dealings, and he took care of business.

Flicka McGurrin

Whatever we got was reasonable. I sort of remember $15 a shift – that seems more or less what we'd get – and then we'd get tips.

Stuart Kremsky

There were a lot of hassles. You didn't get paid very well. But to some extent, you got paid in vibe. You got paid in being able to hang out with Cecil Taylor. You can't put any money on that. You can't eat from that, either. I think a lot of people worked other jobs.

Orrin Keepnews

I was on the scene and privy to all the stories and rumors running around. There apparently were a number of times Todd was having trouble meeting payroll, that musicians were getting paid late. In a couple of cases, he was personally quite friendly with and close to a number of the people that he booked, and the story was that being a good friend of Todd and playing the club meant you might have to wait longer to get paid than somebody he didn't have a personal relationship with. But, again, that's just rumor; nobody came to me and said, "You know what? That son of a bitch didn't pay me for last week."

Eddie Marshall

He paid me.

| **Stuart Kremsky** | It was hard to get paid sometimes because there wasn't any money. Todd would be really good about paying musicians because he was really good to musicians. |

The thing about Todd was that he was so into the music that he couldn't *not* pay the musicians. And musicians would travel on to the next city, and you'd think, "Well, they're out of town. We don't have to [pay them]." But they would get paid. He might pay them late; he might pay them out of next week's money, which meant it kind of barreled on week after week. It was always a struggle. . . . I remember that kind of thing happening with some regularity – not that I had very much to do with the finances. It was a small enough place that you would talk to people and hear, "Oh, they didn't pay him 'til now. . . . Jesus." But if you don't pay musicians, number one, musicians will hear about it and start playing somewhere else.

Dave Liebman

Todd knew well enough – which, of course, any guy who runs a club should know – that you got to reach out and have good relationships with musicians, because that's what makes your club's reputation. If you don't settle with the musicians, you're not going to have a successful place; people aren't going to take it as valid. He was very cool with musicians. They could come in, sit at the bar – whatever. Todd was definitely user-friendly. He knew the guys and he knew enough to keep everybody cool. When you have one place in a town, you got to know how to work the musicians right.

Billy Harper

Most all the musicians who played there liked the vibe. They liked the idea of having that club on the West Coast. They could always go there and really play and have good musicians to play with. It was always a positive thing. At least, you definitely got paid. That's what kind of keeps it as a positive thing with musicians.

Stuart Kremsky

The cool thing was, when you worked there, you could come in any time. You could show up and go into the backroom and check out the gig and hang out at gigs even when you weren't working. I saw a lot of gigs. I was a paying customer before I worked there, and then I really liked working there because I didn't have to be a paying customer. It was cool.

Flicka McGurrin
On my nights off, I used to bring people in all the time. Especially on a Tuesday, Wednesday, or Thursday, which weren't such big nights. And we would never pay the cover charge. Todd would just get so disgusted. He'd say, "How could you do that? It's just so rude. You know, you're so presumptuous." And I would just be so cocky and say, "Well, we're all buying drinks. We all drink a whole lot." We were upping the bar, so I never felt guilty about that.

devorah major
The Keystone Card was a card that I believe cost $20 – maybe $25 – and you could go ten times. At the time on the San Francisco buses, you had bus cards that a kid would buy for fifty cents and it would give them ten rides on the bus. So, it was like that. It was supposed to be nontransferable but, you know, you could get your hand stamped and sneak out and give somebody else your Keystone Card, and [they could] come in. [Laughs]

There was a certain relationship to Keystone, particularly after the Keystone Cards came, where for my set it was, "Do you want to go out dancing? Do you have enough money to go to Keystone and buy a couple of drinks? Or is there a house party?" These were our three evenings. We went to hear jazz, we went to a disco club dancing, or we were at a house party. Or we were home listening to music.

I saw Pharoah Sanders on my Keystone Card three times – in a week. That's what it let you do. You would actually go back again to see the same person that you thought was so great; it made it totally affordable. I think you were supposed to buy two drinks a set, but I don't remember ever being hassled. And we got one drink a set, always, me and my friends. Unless there was some guy that was buying them. Then, we got whatever we wanted: "Oh, I'd like a cognac. I guess I don't want a beer." That was what a Keystone Card was. And 'cause you came so often with a Keystone Card, the people on the door got to know you. It was kind of nice.

Laurie Antonioli
I don't when or how this happened, but I managed to get in for free. That's why the club never made any money. [Laughs] But I would pay, like, half the time, and sometimes I would just stand outside and listen. There was a back door, and you could stand right in there and hear the music pretty well.

Orrin Keepnews

It's been a very important point to me as the years go by to avoid paying door charges like ordinary citizens because, hell, I'm a professional and shouldn't have to do that. Very quickly [in my time at Keystone], it was established that I did not have to pay my way at the club. I was pleased to see that Todd was sufficiently professional for that.

David Williams

I remember it being a Saturday night; Todd remembers it as Sunday. There's a discrepancy. We started the first set. The club was packed. It was summertime; the doors were open and you could see out to the street. I was taking a solo. Elvin [Jones] had left the bandstand and the other guys had left to go take a drink or whatever, so I was up there playing. From the corner of my eye, I could see out to the street and I saw Elvin getting in a cab. [Laughs hard] It was the first set, so I motioned to one of the other guys, I think it was Pat La Barbera, a saxophone player. Roland Prince was the guitar player. They came back, and we just finished whatever it was we were playing, and that was the end of the night. And we never saw Elvin until the next night.

So Todd had to refund people.

Eddie Marshall

When he really got in trouble, his dad would bail him out. His dad was the nicest; they both loved jazz. That's the bottom line with Todd: he really loves jazz music. He would do anything to keep that club open. I mean, the only thing people think Todd figured out was blow [cocaine]. Like, "Aww, man, he was cheating everybody 'cause he was into blow." I said, "Jesus Christ, this is so ridiculous." He was using blow just like everybody else was; it was like a big fad, you know? I don't know anybody now who does cocaine. Maybe I'm out of the mix. Those guys are grown men now and have different lives; they're doing different things. But back then, that's what people did.

Helen Wray

You can't run a club [now] like Keystone was run. They've got to be run as a successful business these days. Maybe that's what made it unique, too. Jazz clubs today, the minimum and the costs are a lot higher. You know, it's funny now how Todd put the ticket up to $8 and people would complain about it 'cause he raised it a dollar. It was ridiculous. [Only] $8 to hear Dexter or Miles Davis or someone.

Flicka McGurrin

And I'm afraid that Keystone Korner, that atmosphere, is kind of gone. I don't think that people are building those kinds of businesses any more. They don't make money, and people go into business to make money. I don't think Keystone ever made money, but it created an incredible stage for fabulous music and great listening.

Todd Barkan business card
Courtesy of George Cables and Helen Wray

KEYSTONE KORNER
Bicentennial Expansion & Survival Concert

GROVER WASHINGTON, JR. SEXTET
GEORGE BENSON QUINTET
& STRING QUARTET
FRIDAY, JANUARY 16, 1976 – 8 PM
PARAMOUNT THEATRE OAKLAND

*Proceeds of Concert to Finance 75 New Seats
& New Ventilation System

Tickets: $5.50, $6.50 & $7.50   at all major outlets

CALL 456-6400 or TELETIX
KEYSTONE KORNER SCHEDULE ATTACHED

Luis Gasca, Lucy Keepnews, Gator, Nancy Swingle,
Todd Barkan, Orrin Keepnews, 1978

Todd Barkan, Charlie Haden, Don Cherry, 1978

Eddie Henderson, Julian Priester, Eddie Marshall, 1978

Rahsaan Roland Kirk, 1977

"Rahsaan." That was really Todd's
inspiration, I do believe.   *George Cables*

They wrote that song "Bright Moments"
together. Todd's name is on that song.   *Eddie Marshall*

Todd Barkan

I met Rahsaan on a bus going to a Columbus Jets game in Columbus, Ohio. He was on his way to see his girlfriend by himself, just with his little stick and his roller at the end of the stick and the horn attached to it. I was about eleven years old. And he became my mentor in the music. It turned out that he lived very close to where I lived in Columbus; the area of town that he lived in, near East High School, was very close to Bexley, Ohio, which is a suburb where my folks lived. My neighborhood was mostly Methodist and Jewish, and he lived in a black neighborhood very close by. His dad owned a candy store. Rahsaan went to the Ohio School for the Blind.

Rahsaan became a mentor to me, and then later on I was able to hire him at Keystone Korner and make the recording of "Bright Moments," which I played keyboards and percussion on. We had a wonderful, life-long relationship. I toured Australia and Europe with Rahsaan during the time that Keystone was open. We toured in '74 and '75, right before he had his stroke. He passed away in 1977.

John Ross

On the Return of Rahsaan Roland Kirk
Keystone Korner, 1976

A hush that cuts right down the dotted line,
A serrated expectancy,
The sun grows dimmer:
Dark moments
Dark moments.
He spills into the room,

His presence incurably fragile.
We have been told that half of him
Is still alive
But which half?
It is escorted to the stage
By zooty bodyguards,
The maze of wire and instruments
Temporarily baffles him
But he penetrates
Without roadmaps or redcaps.
He still knows the footpaths.
Dark moments
Bright moments.
Charcoal clouds part before his moon,
Garlands of sound festoon his collar,
Blindfolds cloak him like a lovely mystery,
Raucous gifts drip from his ponderous lips,
He nonchalantly stuffs six horns into his jaws
Curses the averageness of white bands,
And takes the wanderers
On a weeklong trip
To Ullipia
Returning them each
Wrapped in honey.

There is a formula here, an equation.
It says that if Rahsaan
Is four men simultaneously
Each man 5,000 pounds tall,
That one half of this man
Must be a shining set of twins
Each as heavy as a single Himalaya,
Each as phosphorescent
As the sweet spun ambergris
That rekindles our
Bright moments,
Bright moments.

Ora Harris

When Todd went to Australia with Rahsaan, I think it was one of the happiest times of his life. Not only was he there in Australia with Rahsaan, whom he just adored, but he had the opportunity to also be Rahsaan's eyes. I can remember right now stories of Todd having to move a koala bear for Rahsaan to touch. He was so gentle and sweet with him.

Eddie Marshall

Rahsaan. Rahsaan Roland Kirk. I knew Rahsaan in New York. I happened to grow up in New York at a very great time. I moved to New York in '58 and I left in '66 or '67, so I lived there in some very, very good years. I met a lot of great players before they were famous.

The thing is, this man [Kirk] was totally blind. I worked for years at a club called the Dom at St. Mark's Place. Everybody used to come there to play, and that's how I met Rahsaan. He would leave the club with his saxophones – you can imagine, three or four of them on [his neck] all the time – and a cane. Did you ever see that cane he had? He had these three or four canes all stuck together; he had a horn [Laughs] and a wheel on the bottom. He lived in New Jersey and had to take the PATH train. He'd get on the train by himself, go all the way home, and nobody would mess with him.

One time, he had this big argument at the Dom. It was about free jazz. The Ayler brothers were coming in there all the time. [Marshall imitates their sound:] *Blooo blooo bloo!* And [Rahsaan] didn't like it, and somebody said something to him and Rahsaan got violent. He started fighting. He was this big bull. I mean, he was fearless. [Laughs]

Rahsaan was one of the few guys that ever fired me. His wife would drive us around in a little Volkswagen sedan. And we'd have a set of drums. I don't know how we got all that stuff in there. [Laughs] And we'd go to our gigs. We would travel [locally] to Philly and New York. Anyhow, I worked with Rahsaan and I always told him that I was also traveling across the country with Charlie Mariano and Toshiko. One day, I told him, "I have to leave next month." I gave him a month's notice. "I gotta leave with Toshiko." So the next month comes, and we have this big tour that's going to Japan and everything, and I said, "I have to go. I told you." [Marshall imitates Kirk:] "Aww, man, those in my band supposed to be dedicated." He went out on me. He said, "Man, I can't use you no more. Man, I can't use you." He never called me after that.

When Rahsaan started coming out here, Todd called me [to replace a drummer who could not make the gig], and I said, "Rahsaan and I, we really don't get along any more." He said, "Oh man." And I went. [Rahsaan] didn't even mention it. And we played, and you know it was really nice 'cause – [Whispers] – we used to do acid together. And he got high one time – and he was telling this at the Keystone, too – he said, "Man, I remember one time I got high and I thought I was a penny, and I'm on Times Square, and I'm a penny and all these people are walking by and I'm just a penny laying on the ground and I'm saying 'Hey man,

help me,' and nobody's listening to me." And he totally went into it. . . .
Oh man.

He had a little kid named Rory. Did you know he had a little boy
named Rory?

Flicka McGurrin

Only once – I would say only once; I worked there for five years – did
Todd get up onstage and play "Bright Moments," which was just great.
I've always loved that tune. His love for the music comes out when he
plays that tune. Rahsaan was his guy.

Al Young

I got a big kick out of the night Rahsaan was blowing his siren or, as he
put it, his sireeen, and went into a long harangue about the police station being next door. He said, "Man, I'm sorry but what's this jazz club
doing right up next door to the police station? That's not good. That's
not good, man. I came out here to play some nice jazz music. Police
sitting up there next door. Police and jazz don't go together." He went
on a whole tirade about that. Some nights, I'd see the cops out there
listening to the music.

At the time, there was a guy who had legitimized the police presence in jazz. You remember Lem Winchester, the vibes player [and
former police officer]? A wonderful vibes player; he played like Milt
[Jackson]. His album *Winchester Special*, which I think was on Prestige,
included the tune "Down Fuzz." Jazz DJs loved playing his records; they
used to play it on KJAZ [a Bay Area jazz station no longer in existence].
Because of Lem Winchester's popularity at that time, cops had kind of
a neutralized presence in jazz. It cleaned up the cop image because on
his album he explained where his love for jazz came from. I think he
actually played at Keystone.

Steve Turre

Keystone was always full of inspiring audiences, and Rahsaan had a lot
to do with that. Bill Graham gave him a few gigs to open at the Fillmore,
and he did some gigs at the Fillmore opposite Buddy Guy and some
other San Francisco rock bands. He opened two or three times for rock
bands and blues bands and played with the other bands as well. And all
the hippie kids, man, they realized something beautiful was going on
and they dug it and they became instant fans.

Bill Graham, bless him – I respect him. He knew what real was, and he wasn't scared to present it. He knew that people would respond to real. He'd book Rahsaan with, say, Buddy Guy or the Grateful Dead or something, but Rahsaan did that stuff first. Rahsaan's the one that broke the ground for that kind of experience. Bill Graham saw that that was real and knew the kids would get it. And they did. They responded.

Right about that time, Keystone opened. Rahsaan started playing Keystone, and that whole audience came there and then they just kept coming and hearing the other acts, and a whole generation was brought into the music.

Ora Harris

Rahsaan always wanted to go out after the show to eat, run around San Francisco, and find a place that would be open at two o'clock in the morning where he could sit and eat. And, of course, that always ended up being the International House of Pancakes on Lombard Street. And there would be my son, sitting there, just so happy that he was out with Rahsaan Roland Kirk.

Wynton Marsalis, Art Blakey, 1982

**Working at Keystone, for me, was
like working in a musical library.** *Flicka McGurrin*

Todd Barkan

I'm not as free [now in New York] and the world is not as open as it was at that time. I think we're politically *way* more conservative now than we were in 1972 and especially in the late '60s, when I was really formulating where I was coming from in my musical life, musical vision, ideas about presenting that kind of music. I felt like a very important function of what I did was to educate and broaden the tastes and scope of the musical audience. And I think to this day that the Keystone Korner had an enormous impact on jazz in this country and particularly on what was presented in the Bay Area. And I think in the '70s, I probably had a broader palette.

Steve Turre

Keystone had the commitment not only to the level of artistry and the level of musicianship and creativity but also the commitment to the acknowledgment of the source of the music and the roots of the culture of the music. There are a lot of places all over the country that just don't want to acknowledge the facts of jazz.

For instance, I went to North Texas State for one semester and dropped out. It's supposed to be a so-called jazz school. I don't know what it's like now, but at the time they had all of Stan Kenton's library. They're big-band oriented. They had Basie's library – but only the arrangements written by white arrangers Neal Hefti and Sammy Nestico. It was a complete whitewash. They want you to think white people created jazz. And that's not the truth. Jazz comes from African American culture. It doesn't mean that other people can't play it. How you going to advance the music when you don't know where it's coming from or understand the rhythming foundation of the music?

Keystone stayed true to the source. As a rule, they didn't bring a lot of bullshit artists in there. There's all kinds of jazz: free jazz, bebop, and traditional and big band and fusion. During that time, fusion was Return to Forever and Mahavishnu – all those guys could really play jazz – and they were experimenting with the new sounds of electric instruments. Todd had integrity; if Keystone were open today, they wouldn't be having smooth jazz in there.

Flicka McGurrin

Working at Keystone, for me, was like working in a musical library. Every week, there was new music. We had two to three shifts a week, so that meant we had maybe three hours of music a night – nine hours a week of a certain group, like Horace Silver or Dexter Gordon or Art Blakey.

It was so exciting to hear that music and hear the way the musicians would start out in an evening: the first set, the second set; the third set was always the best. And usually, when you go out at night, you never make it to the third set. Even at Yoshi's, they're always giving the second set away for free, and half the time you don't make it through the second set because you're just tired. But when you work at a place, you hear this fabulous music.

Laurie Antonioli

For a young jazz musician, the greatest gift in the world was to be able to go down there and hear Blakey for five nights in a row, or Horace Silver for five, or Nat Adderley, or Bill Evans – all the people that I heard. I would just camp down there when any of those guys were around.

Carl Burnett

The Jazz Messengers was a way of playing. It established a doorway for young musicians to learn from seasoned musicians the things that they didn't get in school. It was like an education for them. The Jazz Messengers gave them a vehicle to develop their ideas and the lessons that they had learned in school and make it a part of their lives.

Horace Silver had a similar situation; in fact, he was one of the creators of the Jazz Messengers. He brought the young musicians in, and they played Horace's music. They learned to understand the thinking behind it and the presentation of it and see that to play music just of itself sounds one way, but to play it from your heart is another sound.

Art Blakey had more success with it than Horace because the drums are the engine, whereas a piano doesn't have that same kick. Art Blakey would say, "Come on!" and make you play.

Stuart Kremsky   You learned a lot. Working with Red Garland for a week was a real education. I'd never listened to somebody play essentially twelve sets of music. I heard like thirteen or fourteen hours of Red Garland in a week. That's a really strange thing. To Red Garland, that's what he does. But if you're just a fan, you'll typically hear [just] a night here, a night there, but it's another thing entirely to hear set after set after set played by the same guys. So it was real educational on that level. And it was fun.

Helen Wray   I'd heard various albums and been to jazz clubs on and off, but to be there week in, week out, and to hear, say, Dexter play all week and for it still to be new and exciting every single night – you don't get that experience unless you work in those places. To hear Elvin [Jones] for a week, or two weeks even, and every night they're creating something new. . . . It just opens your ears and your mind to a deeper feeling and love for it. You can listen to CDs and albums, but that live experience of those people and the bands that came through was just amazing.

Eddie Marshall   Tito Puente would come there a lot, but one time they had Tito Puente and His Soul Brothers, who were Patato [Valdez], Mongo Santamaria, and Candido – all of those guys playing on the stage together. And at the end of the night, they started talking all that ritual stuff and the ritual Bata drum and all that. It was magic. And it was *really* primitive. The old school Bata drumming. I'm not even familiar with it, but it was just out of this world.

The next week was Cleanhead Vinson. And then you would go to Sam Rivers. And then you'd go to the Fort Apache Band. Betty Carter! You know? Most people out here didn't even know who these people were.

Bob Stewart   It's your job as a promoter, I think, to develop how the music's going and present the music, rather than taking sides. And what [Todd Barkan] did here [at Keystone] was educate his audience. [He booked] Bags [Milt Jackson] playing vibraphone, who was hard bop, and then he'd present Anthony Braxton, who's . . . you know [much more avant-garde]. And if he's doing all that, he's really educating. The audience has a huge range of what they can listen to and comprehend. That's the way they do it quite often in Europe in festivals. They have different styles of things being presented at the same festival, whereas the festivals here in New York . . . it's like you get this [one] segment of the music 'cause [the promoter] figures that's what's going to sell, so they put that segment on. He doesn't set it up to be an educational set.

Not all musicians are able to comprehend different styles of music; they don't know quite what to do. You have to be introduced, you know, to that way of looking at anything. And [in Todd Barkan's case], he's doing that from his stage, and not even as a musician. He's widening his audience's ability to listen by presenting concerts like this.

Helen Wray

We'd have these extraordinary opportunities to have double billings for two weeks of, say, Elvin's band and Max Roach's band. It was extraordinary to hear a band and then hear someone who was equally great. That never happens unless you go to a festival, which isn't really a musical experience; [it's] a fun time where you hear a little music but you're not really listening, you're not really hearing a whole picture.

Carl Burnett

Listening is the key to music, but not everyone knows how to listen. You have to be trained to hear what you might like. If you really listen, you hear the whole structure, and sometimes you like it and sometimes you don't. Those who listened are the ones you found playing together most of the time. That's how they picked people to play in the band, based on the ability to listen.

Keystone was the epitome of listening. All the musicians who came to play there loved it because the people came to listen, and they came religiously – it seemed not to matter who was [performing]. Most of the people were name artists; everybody comes to hear name artists. But the feeling at Keystone was, it didn't make any difference who it was. "We come 'cause we want to hear the music. We're trying to get into the music." It happened in some other places, but the atmosphere wasn't the same.

I think it had to do with the size of the club, number one. The whole focus in there was the stage and the musicians giving of themselves. And those that were there came to give of themselves. And when they did, the people responded and gave back.

Billy Harper

It seemed that people liked coming there, whether they knew much about the music or not. To me, it felt like some of the places I played in Europe: definitely open. Some of those places, even if people are not familiar with the particular artist, they are open for the music, and that's the way it was at Keystone.

devorah major

I knew that I was stretching myself. We knew that we might hear somebody we hadn't heard of because it was no longer on the radio that much. I was a KJAZ fan, but sometimes, to me, KJAZ was boring. They played my father's music. I mean, even though I loved some of my father's music, I wanted to go beyond that.

Whoever they brought in was absolutely worth the listen. And you would leave full. Now, you might not leave having feasted; you might not stay for the second set for all of them; you might not be feeling them that much. But you would never resent the money that you paid. I think that Todd's booking was phenomenal.

Billy Harper

I think each club has its own little personality. In fact, some people in New York who have been owning clubs for a long time actually think they have to have certain people in who fit the club. Well, Keystone Korner had a lot of people who fit the club. It had that progressive kind of feel, but it also felt like some kind of way of educating the public. Informing them. It was not just the typical, traditional kind of thing, but also a broader range. Maybe that's what helped open the minds.

Bob Stewart

I looked upon [Todd Barkan] with the most high regard. Absolutely. In the group with Arthur [Blythe], [my instrument], the tuba, was playing the bass, and most people, first of all, discounted the instrument as playing the bass in those ensembles. So when Todd introduced the band, he spoke about Arthur and the ensemble, and the use of the instruments, and when he spoke about the tuba, he was coming from such a place of knowledge. I was absolutely flabbergasted. He spoke about how this is the original bass, and he said, "This is the instrument that you haven't heard because it didn't evolve like all the other instruments did. It met a ceiling, and they stopped using it. And this gentleman is bringing that instrument back to its original position." I was like, "Whoa . . ." I never heard anybody say that out loud, and it just floored me. To have that kind of knowledge and the kind of sensitivity to express it like that – I was absolutely thrilled.

By 1982, that group of Arthur's had been together for five years or more. We first recorded in '77. And it was the first time that anybody, particularly in a well-known jazz club like the Keystone Korner, had ever introduced me like that. It was just nice to know somebody was paying attention, somebody was listening and had some idea of what I'm trying to do here. He took pains introducing [me].

Jack Hirschman

Barkan did have a communitarian sense, let's put it that way. That was one of the reasons why he was especially fond of booking the liberation gang, Charlie Haden and Don Cherry. These guys were very, very involved. Charlie and Don were among the more conscious people in terms of what was going on outside the world of jazz. Barkan really liked them in the place. That's the reason why, on three or four occasions, we had events [to raise money] for [political] events. We had one in relation to South Africa. Remember when the longshoremen's union refused? We had an event for the South African people's movement. And I remember we had one for the Union of Left Writers, a group that we were involved with. There was also one, I think, for Nicaragua. Todd was really very open to that kind of stuff, even in the midst of all kinds of other *shmegeggy*-ism.

Eddie Henderson

If the Keystone were not there, I would not have had that outlet to play with my heroes. Period. I could have moved to New York, but why? I was practicing medicine, driving Ferraris, and getting a chance to play anyway. It just put icing on the cake. I had my cake and ate it.

Todd did not like *me* at all. At all. I couldn't buy a gig there. The only way I played at the Keystone is because the musicians – Jackie Mac, Elvin [Jones], Art Blakey – they asked for me. Playing with Herbie Hancock gave my credentials validity. I've heard Todd and the cats [in the Bay Area] kinda looked down their nose [at me]: "Oh, he's not a real jazz player. He's a doctor who plays jazz music on the side." Bullshit. Don't get mad at me 'cause I can do multiple disciplines. I heard through the grapevine that Todd said, "Eddie Henderson's a phony because he should sell his Ferrari and give [me] the money to support the Keystone." I said, "Shit, sell my Ferrari? I oughta put you in Napa [State Mental Hospital], motherfucker." [Laughs]

Laurie Antonioli

As a young, developing musician, I had the chance to actually get up onstage a few times with some of the visiting musicians. I got to sit in with Jon Hendricks one time; I sat in once with Tete Montoliu and Pony Poindexter. Sunday nights were when people would be invited. I wasn't ready for my own gig at the Keystone at that time.

Steve Turre

I think the first time I went to Keystone Korner was to see Woody Shaw. I had been on the road with Ray Charles for a year, got back from that, and I heard that Woody had moved out here. Someone said, "Man, you gotta go check him out." So I went down to Keystone and I ended up sitting in with him. I guess that was February of '73, when I had moved back to the Bay Area.

After that, I would always go hang out with Woody, sit in with him. And in April or May of that year, Art Blakey came through town on his way back from Japan, and Woody said he wanted to introduce me to Art. So I sat in, and Art said, "Okay, we're going to be in the studio tomorrow morning at ten o'clock." I said, "What?" He said, "You're in the band now." I said, "What?" I didn't even know any of the tunes; I had just sat in on the blues.

So I get to the studio at ten o'clock, and Orrin Keepnews says, "Man, who is this, Art? Who is this kid with this horn?" Art stood up for me, and he said, "Well, he's in the band now." Orrin didn't know me then. I was struggling back then, trying to learn how to play. I'd have good nights and I'd have other nights where I was still this young kid trying to learn, but Art could hear the potential. And he liked me and that's what counted. Not only did I go back to New York with him, I played the rest of the engagement here at Keystone with him. I was honored to be part of that school. And it all happened at Keystone. If it hadn't been for Keystone, indirectly, I wouldn't be in New York today 'cause that's where it all took place – where I sat in with Art and he asked me to join the group.

[Being a member of Art Blakey's band] was like [attending] a university and a finishing school – a graduate degree in real jazz. And he not only taught you about the music, and how to tell a story, he taught you how to be a man. He taught you how to be a bandleader if you were so destined to be. He'd encourage you when you needed it, and when you got full of yourself he'd bring you back down to earth. He was a hell of a psychologist but, at the same time, a real humanist. One of the most intelligent people I've ever known, I gotta say that. And not just street smarts – total smarts. He's brilliant.

I remember after I played with him that first night and I was sitting there, [Blakey asked,] "Where you going? What are you doing?" I said, "What do you mean?" He said, "Well, you don't play everything you know in the first chorus. Take your time. Tell a story. Take your time and listen to me; I'll take you there." So we'd develop a dialogue, a conversation. You don't have to try and make it happen; you let it happen.

Carl Burnett

Experienced musicians stopped teaching. We never established an institution where we taught what it should be – maybe not necessarily what it *should* be, but what it *could* be for every musician.

Eddie Marshall

Art Blakey is one of my first heroes. He's such a gossiper. He's the one who told me, "Hey, man, Eddie, you know your great-grandfather's in the hospital?" I said, "How do you know my great-grandfather?" "Kaiser Marshall. I told him about you." Kaiser Marshall? I never even heard of Kaiser Marshall. And the fact is I never, ever really heard who my dad's father was. You know what I mean? It was like a taboo question for some reason. But Art Blakey swore that Kaiser Marshall was [my great-grandfather]. I'd have to have some kind of DNA testing or something to really know that.

Kaiser Marshall is a drummer who preceded Art Blakey; he played in Fletcher Henderson's band back in the '20s. He's a good drummer, pretty historic drummer. Some people say he invented the hi-hat. Before, the hi-hat was way down low; it was called the low-hat. And it was just two cymbals that went together, and somebody put it on a stand. I don't know if Kaiser Marshall did it or not, but that's what Art was saying.

Al Young

I was there one night with Don Asher when Jaki Byard was playing. Jaki Byard had been Don Asher's first piano teacher back in Boston, and Don went up to him during a break and said, "You got some new stuff.

I want to learn some of those new things you got going. But I want it at the old price." And so Jaki said, "Okay. If we can find some time, I can show you some stuff. What did I charge you?" "Fifty cents a lesson." He said, "I don't know if I can do that, man."

Laurie Antonioli

There was no other place where you could meet that many great musicians at once. You might find people here and there and around and about, but the Keystone was like a magnet for everybody. I remember sitting back there with Abbey Lincoln one night, and it was quite scary. There was a ton of people back there and all of a sudden everybody left, and I was in the backroom alone with Abbey Lincoln. And I had no idea what to say. I've had this experience a few times with some of the great singers – you know, young white girl with one of the absolute legends of the music – and I could tell she just didn't feel like talking. She made it clear, and I could see she wasn't having a good night for some reason. We're human beings, you know? I didn't bother her. And that was a lesson.

Dave Liebman

I was younger than some of the musicians that played there – Rahsaan, Dexter – but to be able to be part of that was a privilege; it was fantastic. I had a band, Lookout Farm, after I'd been with Elvin and Miles, and we had some measure of success. But to be able to play every night, have the chance to work the music out, think about it, talk about it the next day, change things, and rehearse – that's something that you really need. We're in a period where that doesn't happen any more.

And the music grew when you played in a club with a conducive atmosphere, with an owner that was encouraging, with an audience that was accepting, with equipment that was at least passable if not better. The music has a chance to expand. What we do needs to be worked out. We can't do our stuff in a laboratory, in a rehearsal hall at three o'clock in the afternoon, in a school classroom. That's what it's become now, but you need that ambiance, the looseness, and the kind of jazz attitudes for the music to develop.

Max Roach,
1977

Tootie Heath,
Yusef Lateef,
1977

Elvin Jones band:
Ryo Kawasaki,
Chico Freeman,
Elvin Jones, Jiunie Booth,
Dave Liebman, 1977

Billy Harper, Mickey Tucker, 1977

Pharoah Sanders, 1982

Flora Purim, 1978

Bobby and Bags: Milt Jackson, Eddie Marshall, Bobby Hutcherson, James Leary, 1977

9

He just hits one note. He crushed me with one note.

Eddie Marshall quoting Bobby Hutcherson on Milt Jackson

Stuart Kremsky

The thing about Keystone, and what I think Todd's greatest skill was, was putting together interesting combinations of musicians. Nobody else would put Max Roach and Art Blakey on the same bill, but Todd did that.

Todd Barkan

I put lots and lots of bands together. I mean, that's part of what I do and what I've done for the last thirty years. I do it here [in New York] at Dizzy's. And I did it there in the '70s – put bands together. I'm the one that put George Cables with Charles McPherson.

Putting Bobby Hutcherson and Milt Jackson together was something that I just wanted to do for many years. I knew [from] Bobby that Milt was his hero, number one, and I knew that Milt was often very resistant about the idea of playing with another vibes player. That took quite a long time to happen. Milt Jackson had to approve it because Milt was the boss. Bobby was only one of his children. One of his progeny. Now, Bobby is the boss and Stefon Harris and Joe Locke are his children. Generations. I suggested that [they perform together] three or four times before it happened. And even the week that it happened, it wasn't supposed to happen. Milt said, "*No.*" Then, finally, in the middle of the week, he said, "Man, have Bobby come in." And, of course, I didn't have to bend Bobby's arm; Bobby wanted to do it from the very beginning. So Bobby came, and it was a great thing.

Eddie Marshall

Todd had hired Bobby Hutcherson and Milt Jackson to showcase the week, and I'll never forget how nervous Bobby was. It was very funny; he was so nervous to play with Milt Jackson. He'd seen him playing plenty of times – you used to always see Milt – but that was the first time he played with him. Bobby would play a barrage of notes and Milt Jackson would go *biing!* And that used to knock Bobby out. [Laughs] "He just hits one note. He crushed me with one note."

I'll never forget my first rehearsal with Milt Jackson. I had my little hippie set of drums and it was really raggedy. They were a set of drums that I didn't like the color of, so I took all the sparkle stuff off – it was just all natural wood that I painted – and I took the heads off 'cause I was looking for some other kind of sound that was somewhere between funk and jazz. I don't know what it was; I don't know what I was thinking.

Anyhow, I had come to rehearsal and I had a ride cymbal that had a lot of tape on it, and Milt says to me [Marshall imitates Jackson's raspy voice], "What's all that tape?" [Laughs] I said, "I have to have it on there because the cymbal's too loud," and he said, "I don't play tape. I don't like that sound, the tape. Take that tape off."

Now, what was I going to do? This is Milt Jackson. Normally, I would have been really arrogant and said something really smart. I said [Marshall speaks in a soft voice, as if to himself], "Damn, this is Milt Jackson. What am I talking about?" You know? So I take the tape off. He knew instinctively that if I had tape on that cymbal, I was gonna be banging the fuck out of it because it's like, "I'm just loose. I'm San Francisco. We play loud." And he knew I couldn't do that if I took the tape off. So I had to really control the cymbals. And to this day, I don't put tape on, and if I do put tape on a cymbal, it's for recording purposes or something, but *never* [at a gig].

George Cables

I remember doing Eddie Marshall's record *Dance of the Sun* with him. That was great to play with him because he could play. He was a good writer, and he plays the recorder – and I don't mean tape recorder. He plays great. We got to play a lot together with Bobby. And I remember Bobby's vibes. Sometimes, he'd have to hold them together with a rubber band. He'd be putting them together and they'd be falling apart. [Long laughter]

Keystone was a special place for Bobby. I remember making a lot of good music with Bobby. We made a lot of records together too. Bobby knows a lot of my compositions, a lot of my pieces. We played a lot of my music and just developed a kind of musical relationship that was special – should I say "symbiotic"? Yeah! That's exactly what happened. I enjoyed giving, playing. I learned a lot from Bobby. I really relate to what he does, what he was doing. I think it was something special with Bobby and Milt. That's his musical father: Milt Jackson.

Bobby Hutcherson, 1977

Milt Jackson, 1977

Milt Jackson,
Bobby Hutcherson,
1977

Courtesy of George Cables
and Helen Wray

Dexter Gordon, 1977

10

> **How could you not fall in love**
> **with Dexter Gordon?**
>
> *Eddie Marshall*

Ronnie Matthews

When Maxine [Gordon] got Dexter to come back [from Europe in 1973], there was a group with Woody Shaw, Junior Cook, Stafford James, and me. And so Maxine put Dexter with us – the opening salvo, so to speak – just to reintroduce him to America. Then, shortly after that, Dexter got his own group.

Todd Barkan

We put things together; that's part of what we do as jazz club owners. Or you try to do that. They don't just put themselves together. It's a community effort; it's an industry effort. You work with booking agents, managers, artists. . . . It always has to be based on the music. The music has to come first for these things to work at all. You know, some bass players like playing with other drummers better. You don't put them together like you're putting chess pieces on a chessboard. Or like you would Parcheesi tiles on a Parcheesi board. It's based upon the nuances and idiosyncrasies and the symbiotic relationships of one jazz musician and another. The reason that the quartet works with George Cables, Rufus Reid, Eddie Gladden, and Dexter Gordon has to do with both their personal feelings and personal idiosyncrasies as people first, as well as their ability to get along. On the bandstand, Dexter was far behind the beat, and George Cables was ahead of the beat, and Rufus Reid and Eddie Gladden would flow back and forth – and that's what made the whole pendulum work. That was the Dexter Gordon Quartet. It was Dexter's overall *whahh* that carried the whole thing forward, but the elements were based upon the tongue-and-groove of Rufus Reid and Eddie Gladden swinging so hard, George Cables being slightly in front of the beat, Dexter Gordon being behind the beat. That's what made that whole group have so much swing and such intensive propulsiveness.

George Cables   I remember when I played with Dexter – I don't know if this was the first time I played with Dexter there or not, but the marquee said, "Max, Dex, Hutch." That was a Christmas/New Year's week, a hell of a celebration. First, I'd play with Bobby [Hutcherson]; Bobby came on first. Then, Max [Roach] would come on with his piano-less band. And then, I'd come back and play [with Dexter]. The whole week! That was wonderful.

Helen Wray   You knew that Dexter was always going to drink you out of cognac, the Courvoisier, and that you'd have to run down to Coit Liquors in the middle of the set and buy another bottle or two, 'cause he'd drink us out of it.

Al Young   Dexter had a bad habit of just grabbing people's drinks off the table. If there was a full glass, he would take a sip. So [one evening], he was thirsty, and he reached for what he thought was a glass of water, and I think it was vodka, pure straight vodka on ice, and he took a long pull of it, then he put it down and looked at the guy and said, "Uuuggghhhh," and he made this funny face and went right on playing.

Flicka McGurrin   One night, I was there with my friend Lena, and we were two of maybe seven people in the audience because Dexter was supposed to play that night but they couldn't get him to come to the club. And so they had to refund everybody's money and everybody had more or less walked out, except for a few diehards who actually believed that they could eventually get him to come.

Dexter finally walked in the door, and each of his musicians – Eddie Gladden, Kirk Lightsey, and one other – they were all kind of at a standoff. They were all in corners of the room, and you could hardly see them because it was so dark and the stage was empty. I didn't really know the workings of the musicians that well, so I didn't know how much animosity had been caused. But everybody was obviously pissed. And so Lena and I just started clapping. And we started clapping, clapping, clapping, and we didn't let up. We eventually clapped all the guys back up on the stage. And they played. We felt, of course, really proud of ourselves. They played and they played.

I think it cost $8 to get in [the club]. I would be pretty upset if I was the person hiring them and I was out fifty to a hundred people's $8.

Helen Wray   Todd told me about Dexter being there one night and somebody stepped on his foot, and he said, "My shoes are dirty, but my soul is clean."

Al Young   I remember the night that Dexter didn't show and Todd tried to stave off the audience for hours. People were there for the early show, and Dexter didn't show up until about 11:30 at night. I got the backstory from Gretchen Horton. Todd had told Gretchen his half of the story, and she told it to me.

What had happened was, the night before Dexter and Todd had gone to Todd's apartment where Dexter listened to recordings of his going back to the beginning of his recording career in the '40s. Todd had an incredible collection. He had all these things of Dexter's that [Dexter] hadn't heard. So they stayed up all night and the next day listening to records.

Todd had dropped Dexter off at a grocery store and then gone up to crash at his place. Dexter had gone to his hotel, and for all [Todd] knew, Dexter was still asleep. Todd got up on the stage and everybody was rebelling and wanted their money back, and he said, "Wait wait wait wait wait. Cool it! Cool it. You guys are such hypocrites 'cause I've seen you wait around here for a lot of stuff that's not as significant as Dexter, and you don't complain at all." Somebody said: "Like what, Todd?" Todd said, "Like a little dope. You guys will wait two weeks for a little dope. But you can't wait for Dexter."

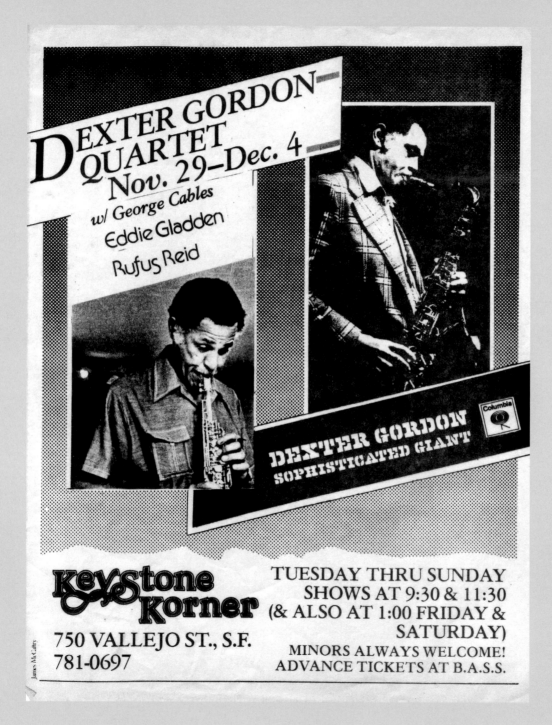

Eddie Gladden, 1980

Dexter Gordon, George Cables, 1977

Dexter Gordon, 1977

Bobby Battle, Sam Rivers, Dave Holland, 1977

11

**They never asked Sam Rivers down
to the Vanguard, you know?**   *Bob Stewart*

George Cables

Keystone was such a special place. There was the Both/And. There was the [Jazz] Workshop. The Both/And was probably more hang-friendly; you could hang there with people that you got to know. And Keystone, [when] you got to Keystone, that was sort of like the crown, the jewel of all the places. For me and [musicians of] my era, going into Keystone Korner was something special.

David Williams

Most club owners I've encountered and worked for, even the ones who knew something about the music, didn't have the passion that Todd had. It was kind of rare for a club owner to have that. With a lot of other club owners, there's separation; with Todd, you almost forgot that he was not part of the band.

Todd Barkan

There have been other environments in the history of the music that have been comparable [to Keystone]. There was a certain era of the Village Vanguard when that was true in New York City, and at Bradley's in New York City, and there have been other clubs around the world, spots where musicians and the people running the club seem to be on the same page. When the musicians came to that environment, they felt that not only somebody cared but that everybody cared. And that's part of what made the music happen on the level that it did and with the consistency that it had.

Clubs have a very strong tendency to take after the personality and the ethos of their owners. One of the reasons that the Vanguard was as wonderful a club as it was at one time was the man who started it, Max Gordon. He was there every night. He cared. He was a gruff and non-romantic-speaking guy, and he was certainly no hippie-dippy. He was in there smoking a cigar and minding his business, but he was a great supporter and idealist of the music. An aesthete. He knew what the hell he was doing; he was a great club owner and he treated me very much like an adopted son. He and I conferred all the time. He got advice from me and I got an enormous amount of advice from him. And likewise, Bradley Cunningham at Bradley's created a warm environment that reflected as much of Bradley as anything else. So I think Keystone had some of my personality in it, and I was able to imbue some warmth and love into the room, and that's what I'm trying to do here at Dizzy's too, twenty years later.

I'm proud of all that because I think that's part of my legacy. In the Bay Area, Yoshi's is part of my legacy just as Keystone was. And it's a continuation of that legacy because so much of what they do, I did in the '70s. It's almost no different, you know, just a little more diluted. It's not quite as pure a programming but, by and large, it's basically in the same vernacular with the same artists.

Ronnie Matthews

Until the Lincoln Center club opened, probably the club that paid the most money was the Blue Note. But the Blue Note, even though it has an after-hours jam session and all that, doesn't give you the same kind of musician-friendly atmosphere or feeling that you would get in a Keystone or Bradley's. A place like Keystone or like Bradley's might give you a drink once in a while.

Do I want to talk about the drugs? That's not what the place was about. You know, there were a lot of people who were using drugs. I guess there were certain clubs all over the country where maybe you could go in the basement or something and do what you had to do. I never thought of the drug scene as being one of the highlights. The music – it was about the music.

Orrin Keepnews

It was very hard to compare the two clubs [San Francisco's Great American Music Hall and Keystone Korner] because the Music Hall was a much bigger room; you could draw a lot more and make a lot more, but you also could have acts rattling around in it. Tom Bradshaw [the owner] was not always terribly successful, but [he] was trying to be a businessman who was running a club, which happened to be a club that booked jazz acts. Whereas with Todd, you always got the feeling that he was a guy running a jazz club, which is, more than semantically, a very different set of circumstances. Fundamentally, for much of the decade, those two clubs were going their separate ways. But my point about Todd was that I never thought of him as a club owner who had a club with jazz in it. I thought of him as a jazz person who was running a club. And I think there were times when he did a rather inept job of running the club, but you never could fault his spirit or his intentions.

Ronnie Matthews

I don't know, business-wise, how Todd handled the club. I don't know anything about that. I really don't. I'm just saying that he was a very relaxed dude who was there having a good time with everybody else. And enjoying the music and the musicians. That's definitely atypical. The only other place I could kind of compare it to as far as that aspect is concerned is Bradley's when that was open here in New York. Bradley [Cunningham] was, you might say, a frustrated piano player, for lack of a better term. He was really into the music himself. He liked to sit down at the piano once in a while, and he started the joint as a piano duo, bass and piano. He loved the music and the musicians and hanging out and having fun. Many times, the doors would close at four o'clock [in the morning] and we'd be in there until the sun came up, having fun, playing piano, everybody taking turns. That kind of interaction between the club owner and the musicians – Todd had that kind of a thing going, too. It was more like he was one of the guys than the club owner. I mean, he was right there with us. Some places are uptight and other places are very relaxed, and most of the other places are somewhere in between.

George Cables

I can remember staying there [at Keystone Korner] after hours 'til sometimes four o'clock, six o'clock, eight o'clock in the morning. Talking, hanging out, maybe playing a little bit, comparing notes, hanging with George Mraz, with Roy Haynes. It was just a musical haven, 'cause there was something special – a really special energy. I can't think of any other place offhand. I mean, there were great places like the Village Vanguard. The Vanguard is still here, still alive, still going. If those walls could talk, or be played back, if they could just play back the things that they heard, that could be amazing. The musicians that I've heard there! But for me and for my era, I think the Keystone was probably *the* jazz club because of the feeling and the vibe that the musicians had, and the audience who came to hear this music. All kinds of people were there.

Helen Wray

I think everyone misses Bradley's. Musicians miss Bradley's like they miss Keystone. I suppose musicians felt a lot the same about Bradley's because it is where they went after work and saw everyone they knew, everyone that hung there. "Oh, let's go to Bradley's and see who's there." It's slightly different, but in New York I know [that] the clubs they like are the ones where the staff seems to have an understanding of what [the musicians] are doing. The Jazz Standard's pretty good, and Birdland.

I guess the Vanguard in New York is like that. It's a funky little place but people are drawn to it. You hear the trains going by, and it's another one of those places that everyone, all the greats, has played at. Somehow, it impregnates the walls to give it that special feeling. Maybe Keystone was like that too. We often used to say, "Boy, if these walls could speak, what stories they could tell."

Clubs in New York will do a Thursday through Sunday or a Friday through Sunday unless it's somebody like McCoy, and he will bring in people for a whole week. Todd did it whether they would bring in people or not. He would still have them for a week. He knew some nights they weren't going to make it.

Billy Harper

New York had, at that time [in the '70s], interesting clubs. For example, the Vanguard was kind of small, actually, downstairs. A lot of clubs seemed to have that idea of going downstairs. In Europe, they have a lot of clubs where you always have to go downstairs into the dungeon, sort of. [Laughs] The Village Vanguard's not quite like a dungeon, but it is going downstairs. Keystone Korner was up, like a West Coast thing. I like the idea. They had good musicians come by. It felt like California. It didn't feel like New York.

Eddie Marshall

You know, Keystone was a special place to come for these [East Coast] guys 'cause there was no place like that in L.A.; [Los Angeles] has a different atmosphere. Except for the really, really high ceiling, Keystone could have been a New York club. In all the clubs in New York, the ceilings are like this, ya know? [Moves his hand low] Keystone was like this. [Moves his hand high]

Steve Turre

Keystone was comparable with any of the great jazz clubs on the East Coast. During the time that the Keystone was there, there was nothing else on the West Coast that had the vibe. There wasn't anything in L.A. that compared to Keystone Korner. Nah. Certainly wasn't Catalina's. Nah. Todd brought in the highest-quality jazz, the real music; he brought in the real shit. He was consistent with it and kept it alive, and sometimes he had to bite the bullet, but he still kept the music coming. Most importantly, *he* believed in the music.

Carl Burnett

San Francisco was the East Coast of the west. For the musician, it was like home because it was a city. L.A. wasn't a city. It was like a big, old, sprawled-out country town. Not even a country town because everything was too spread out. The Lighthouse was in Hermosa Beach, Shelly's Manne-Hole was in Hollywood, Concert by the Sea was in Redondo Beach. Everything was all spread out.

In New York, you could go to any club. All of them were close. The energy was there. The people were there. It was easy to find a certain kind of energy no matter where you went. San Francisco was similar because it was a city. Even though there weren't many clubs, people had recollections of the Jazz Workshop; you heard people talk about the Blackhawk [and] the Both/And. The Both/And was a similar energy to Keystone because of the way it was run.

devorah major

Koncepts is the last club I can think of where you could just buy a ticket and know it would be worth the price of admission. Even the S.F. Jazz Festival, [where] I work as an artist-in-residence, I'm not feeling everybody they bring out. Not that they're not good. I can't say that. Everybody is good. But it's not just "Is everybody good?" It's "Is everybody going to touch your heart?" I think everybody always in some way touched my heart at Keystone Korner. And maybe that was youth, too, because I wasn't at all calcified.

George Cables

In Todd's office, we could close the door and not deal with the riffraff, 'cause it seemed like everybody in the Bay Area wanted to get in the backroom. I remember in the Both/And, the dressing room was the size of a small closet. And you'd go in there and do whatever you had to do that you couldn't do out in the open, and the next thing you know, *knock knock knock*, "It's Joe," *knock knock knock*, "It's so-and-so." It was their room. You were just a musician; you were just there borrowing the room while you were there.

Bob Stewart

Look at the audience. Far out. That's not what an audience looked like at a jazz club in New York at the time. These kind of folks, kind of like on the hippie side, wouldn't be at the Vanguard. [Sighs] '77. I was there [at the Vanguard] with Gil Evans. It's more of a tourist place [now] while at the same [time] a regular New York jazz audience goes there. But it's so expensive.

Ronnie Matthews

In a place like Keystone, you might have – I'm trying to choose my words here – I don't want to say "hippie," but more free-thinking, progressive-thinking people who are thinking about coming together rather than being rugged individualists. But the jazz audience is an audience that is composed of all kinds of people. To me, it's the great democracy – on and off the bandstand – 'cause you have this cross-section of people, even at the big jazz festivals and such. You don't have riots like you have at rock festivals. [Laughs] Uh uh. People are more open and friendly to each other. So you might have a little more of that type of person in the Keystone.

George Cables

In Seattle, I played at the Jazz Alley, the original one in the U District, and I was relaxed. People just walked in and looked around, and you knew you were going to have a good time. The people who ran the place were already on your side. It wasn't about "You got to do this and that by this time." That comes with the territory. "You have to do some of this." There was some of that, but it was really relaxed. Because it was in the U District, people would come in casual dress. But there were other people who would come in dressed. [Pulls on imaginary tie] So there was room for everybody.

The second place John Dimitriou had opened was in the Pioneer Square area, another Jazz Alley. I played there one time, and as I remember, I walked in and it was really sort of elegant and a little overwhelming in that way – these big columns and maybe marble floors in the foyer. And all of a sudden, I felt a sense of, "Ooooo, how am I supposed to act? Do I have to wear a tie?" (which I probably wouldn't have worn anyway). But it's another feeling, and it's got to affect you. If you go in with your program, I don't think you drastically tailor your program to fit the room, but it definitely can change how you play.

I try to always play the same way or play whatever's on my mind, and at Keystone, I'd feel more relaxed about playing. I might be a little apprehensive in some places, at first, because some rooms bring in different audiences. It affects how you feel. And, you know, with jazz – especially small group jazz – it's music of the moment because it's improvised music. So, every day, things change. Even if you play the same repertoire, the same songs, the music is changing. And it depends upon who is playing, too. There are some people who are more affected [by a club's environment], some people that just don't care.

In some places, you're aware of minding your p's and q's, and some rooms change with the different audiences. But, I might as well say it now: I don't necessarily look for or favor a jazz-aficionado audience over one that's maybe just people who are there to hear music. I do like that honest ear that comes with nothing, with no preconceptions. Those are very valuable because you're reaching people. You reach out to people, and Keystone was great for that. People who came there, I thought, were fairly knowledgeable about music, or they liked jazz, but they were *ready* to hear some music. And that was great. That's what you want.

Billy Harper

In New York clubs, if they were established, you were expected to be a little bit more formal, even if you didn't dress formal. It's like that now at some of the clubs in New York. Iridium feels like a much more strict business kind of feel. When you get into Lincoln Center, it's another thing. [Laughs] But, you know . . .

At Keystone, even if you weren't tuned in yet, you could kind of meld with the audience and get there in a relaxed way. It made it easier for musicians to get into their music and what they're trying to do; they're much more able to be more expressive – unless you are really such a professional that you are going to tune everything out and get there anyway. I have to approach a lot of places that way: no matter what is happening there, you have to be able to tune in and let the other stuff go.

[At Keystone], it felt like when you're at a real jazz concert outside – relaxed and sitting on towels outside but really into the music, that kind of thing – but this was inside.

Calvin Keys

If you didn't work Keystone, you weren't in the game. Keystone Korner in San Francisco was like the Village Vanguard is to New York: one of the few places that was left during that time where you could hear any top jazz artist, which is saying somethin'. I mean bebop. I'm not talkin' about smooth jazz; I'm talking about some hardcore. Wayne Shorter on back. Herbie Hancock. I mean, everybody played Keystone Korner. It was a mecca. It was a place where the musicians held meetings, musical meetings. Todd was hip enough to want to have the real music live.

Ronnie Matthews

It had its own character that was not like any other club. The Vanguard is unique; it's the oldest club in the world. It's been open for over sixty years continuously [since 1934]. That's quite a run. Joe Siegel in Chicago – he's moved around, had a few different spots. He's maintained for a long time. And longevity in itself is unusual when it comes to clubs like that.

But each place is a unique spot and that is directly due to whoever owns the place. Right here in New York, Bradley's was unique, and it was because of Bradley, ya know? And so, once he passed on and his wife took over, it had to change; it could never be that again. It had that stamp on it. And I guess, in that sense, Keystone had Todd's stamp on it. The Vanguard, too, when Lorraine took over after Max died, the atmosphere changed a little bit. And Joe Siegel, even though he's been in, well, three different locations over the years, he himself sets up a kind of atmosphere.

Carl Burnett

I remember talking to Herbie Lewis and he said, "When I come to San Francisco, I can be an adult." Every place else, he felt like people didn't give him the proper respect.

Eddie Henderson

The Both/And, Jazz Workshop, Blackhawk, Bob City, the Vanguard – clubs all over the world – Keystone was no different. It was just a jazz club. Let's not try to make it any more than that. It was a jazz club in San Francisco that everybody loved. When Art Blakey or Miles would come there, they'd go to the basement or the back office; they do that all over the world. They have kitchens, with [chefs like] Ora cooking the food, all around the world. You know, they got fine ladies coming in; they got ugly ladies coming in; they got bulldaggers; they got ho's. It wasn't any different than anywhere else. Write that in the book.

Orrin Keepnews

Jazz has never been in very good shape as far as what goes on in the clubs. As far as jazz performance in New York is concerned, you had always a couple or three long-range survivor clubs. You were never aware of, "Gee, jazz isn't doing that well," because you always had Birdland, which was sitting there, in a wonderful location at Broadway and Fifty-Second Street, and had headline acts and had big prices and worked. Other clubs came and went but the fact of the matter is, it wasn't just jazz clubs that came and went. It was just anything. I was not aware at the time [in the '70s] of jazz being in any worse shape than its average shape. So, if it was disco that was beating it up at that point, then five years before it had been something else, and five years later it would be something else.

San Francisco, let's face it, has never been the nightlife city that it would like to be considered. In San Francisco through the '70s, you had as a bare, irreducible minimum one club that was thriving. And there were others that came and went during that period, but Keystone was the standout club. It lasted, and what I'm really saying is that a sort of boy-wonder club owner ran a jazz club that survived for basically a decade in not the biggest and not the hippest city in the world. And I think that says good things all around.

Flora Purim, 1978

Eddie "Cleanhead" Vinson, 1979

Elvin Jones, Chico Freeman, Dave Liebman, 1977

Ron Carter, 1976

Ted Curson, 1979

Cedar Walton, Art Farmer, 1977

I always wore my little crazy hippie stuff. It was California! Definitely wasn't New York.

Eddie Marshall

Todd Barkan

Sometimes, people had bands that got together in New York and came out, but I was able to put a lot of bands together, like the band that eventually became the Timeless All-Stars: Harold Land, Curtis Fuller, Bobby Hutcherson, George Cables, Buster Williams, Billy Higgins. That was a combination of East Coast–West Coast, and they came together at Keystone. Roy Haynes and George Cables joined forces at the Keystone Korner, with Bobby Hutcherson, and they recorded at Fantasy. Red Garland, Ron Carter, Philly Joe Jones – likewise. Orrin Keepnews really put that together.

George Cables

I considered myself an East Coast musician even though I'd been living in Los Angeles for several years. But as far as the concept of playing jazz, I felt that I was more akin with the people from the East Coast. I was born here [in New York]. The attitude in the music was a little more high energy, and I think I was very much a part of that – in my spirit, in my attitude, in my New York musical attitude – although I don't think I wanted to *be* a New York pianist, or even a West Coast pianist. I don't want to be limited by those terms. But in the positive sense, I had a New York attitude.

Eddie Marshall

I always wore my little crazy hippie stuff. It was California! Definitely wasn't New York. Before I moved to California, almost every gig I played, from the time I was fourteen, I wore a suit. Every one, a suit and a tie, 'til I moved out to the West Coast. That's the way it was.

I remember when Horace [Silver] came out here, everybody was dressed. Art Blakey's band? They were always sharp until the very, very end. The Modern Jazz Quartet – impeccably dressed. Everybody, except maybe when people were wearing dashikis. When I left [New York] in the '60s, that's what was happening. A lot of brothers were wearing dashikis and stuff. But for the most part, you dressed up. It all changed in California. The guys, except for Dexter and some people, they had a chance to *not* wear suits and dress up.

Dave Liebman

There is always an aberration that can exist for a while – that's a place out of time. It happens. Keystone was sort of like that in the sense that it brought a really New York vibe into San Francisco. It was tinged with a San Francisco vibe, which was nice, but it was a jazz club, a serious jazz club. [Todd] built an audience, and he did a great job. But you can't exist in one place [where there is only one major jazz club]. A local musician can't. It's not right 'cause everybody depends on it. It gets heavy for the guy owning it. Who's going to work there? It gets more complicated than it appears.

In New York, people are driven – *were* driven – to hear jazz because of the conditions of life there. It's not a war zone, but there are stresses, and you're hearing music 'til two in the morning. Then, you take a taxi home, or you walk home, and you're in a vibe. That didn't happen here [in San Francisco]. Of course, I had to be here to see that. I enjoyed my year and a half here very much. I was living in a houseboat right there near that bridge. I absolutely loved the city. But it was not a city for real deep, deep, passionate feeling and funky vibe. In the end, there really isn't that kind of vibe of necessity.

I came here [to San Francisco] 'cause I really loved the city. I didn't think about career or anything like that. I thought I could do better here than on the East Coast for a variety of reasons. It worked out for a while. But I was in the middle of burning. It wasn't a place you could stay. Not for the music we play.

People have to support it. You need a massive population, first of all. And you need cultural diversity. You need a lot of students and artists around in close proximity to support the music. This doesn't happen any more 'cause they can't afford it. But in those days, your audience really was made up of fellow musicians and artists, people who loved that life, who were serious about their work, who saw jazz as part of what their lifestyle was just like they saw art and painting. You need certain numbers. It's almost a heat: you need a certain degree to get the heat up. It can't be a small coterie of people. It will not exist. You need hundreds, thousands, a couple of million. And this place couldn't support it. When

I saw Eddie Henderson, Julian Priester, and guys like that have a set for eight people . . . it's not right. [I thought,] "This music doesn't belong here." In the end, we left.

I can understand guys staying 'cause every city has guys who stay, who are icons in the city. Every city in America has that. And you need those guys to support the young musicians. They support guys like us if we come in to play and they are part of the community and they made their roots here. They just love living here. It's more important to be living here than to be in a situation that's not livable for their personality or their economics or whatever situation. Both Eddies [Eddie Moore and Eddie Henderson] and George [Cables], when you were in San Francisco, you knew they were there. And that all came out of the Keystone experience.

Eddie Marshall

I grew up on the East Coast, but most of the jazz musicians I met in New York all came from different areas – half of them from California. All my good friends, like Billy Higgins, Dexter, and even Mingus – they were all from California. I didn't even know they had black people out there. I used to ask them, "Are you guys cowboys?" [Laughs]

I met Ed Kelly in New Haven, Connecticut. I was working in a group with Houston Person, and Ed Kelly would sit in at the organ. He was this mild-mannered guy. He's always really nice, and he could play better than almost anybody there. And so I got to meet him: "Hey, man. Where you from?" He said, "I'm from Oakland, California." I said, "I didn't know they had black people in California." Then I moved out here, maybe ten years later, and I got to meet his family. He's still the nicest guy. [Editor's note: Ed Kelly passed away in 2005.]

Steve Turre

I know on Mondays, or sometimes Monday and Tuesdays, if [Todd] had a five- instead of a six-night run, he'd have local people in there. The Moffett family used to play there regularly. Ed Kelly played there regularly. He'd give people a shot. Unfortunately, there's this thing: if you're from New York, you're a New York musician, but if you live in New York, there's no such thing as a New York musician. Either you can play or you can't, and you work or you don't. But outside of New York, you're a local musician or you're a New York musician. So, once I moved to New York, I had to be there a good fifteen years before I got respect at home. If you live here, you're just a local musician: you don't get choice gigs, you don't get paid the same, you don't get the same respect. It doesn't matter what level you play on. And that's not right. It's not Keystone; it's just the way it is outside of New York. I got issues with that stuff. Look at Faye Carol. She's outta sight. If she went to New York, she'd be famous, but she never did. She wanted to stay here and raise her family. Ed Kelly, too. It's just how it is.

New York has always been the hub of the wheel, the epicenter of jazz, since maybe the '30s. And it still is. People are a lot more lazy on the West Coast, especially L.A. They didn't want to work that hard. They're used to coasting. Also, the West Coast school is cool. They don't play with the same energy, the same vitality. Once you got it, you got it. I could see where it's easy to get lazy out here 'cause it's so beautiful. I grew up here. But I was motivated and I felt like I was penalized here for playing vigorously, for playing with all my heart, for playing with determination. So I left, and look what happened. I did good. I'm not sorry I left, but I love it here. It's so beautiful.

Eddie Marshall

The people that [Todd] presented and different styles – just the top jazz artists from everywhere! It wasn't just a total bebop room, ya know what I mean? It was my main introduction to Latin music. That's one thing I like about the West Coast. I lived on the East Coast all my life. I never knew any Chinese Americans; I never knew any Puerto Rican Americans. Everybody'd be in their own little bag, ya know? And I didn't really hear their music or anything. One of the greatest clubs [the Palladium] was right around the corner from Birdland.

I got out here and moved to L.A. where I met these Mexican guys from East L.A., like Ray Vargas, Ray Bohegas, and this trumpet player, Felix Rodriguez. These guys could play their asses off – and living in East L.A. Then I came up here [to San Francisco] and I met John Jang, Chinese American cat; I played music with and met people from the Asian Art Center. I'm meeting all of these people from all these different backgrounds, [and we're] all playing jazz music, you know? Tito Puente and the Fort Apache Band. Mongo Santamaria. Airto used to tear that place apart. Some amazing music. So there's that about Keystone.

Freddie Hubbard, Percy Heath, Jimmy Heath, 1978

Hilton Ruiz, Herbie Lewis, George Coleman, Eddie Moore, 1979

Randy Weston, 1978

Leon Thomas, 1978

I remember Keystone Korner in these early days, and, you must remember, I come from New York; I am a jazz person. *Orrin Keepnews*

Orrin Keepnews

First of all, to set the time context, I got to San Francisco in October 1972 and I came out here specifically to work for Fantasy Records, which at that time had just acquired all the masters that had originally been Riverside Records. Fantasy was a San Francisco–based, very esoteric, mostly jazz label, although Lenny Bruce was one of their biggest items. That's where Dave Brubeck started. And that label was taken over by a guy, Saul Zaentz, who had been the office staff and sales manager there. He had decided to take a chance with the band of the kid in the mailroom: John Fogarty. The band was Creedence Clearwater, which became the biggest thing [in the music industry]. Suddenly, Fantasy found itself with all the money in the world and, possibly the first time this had ever happened, used it to further their devotion to jazz.

I had been one of the founders of Riverside and I had done virtually all of the producing. All of the key names that you associate with Riverside – [Thelonious] Monk, Cannonball [Adderley], Bill Evans, Wes Montgomery, Johnny Griffin, Jimmy Heath – all of that was part of New York Riverside. The company went out of business in 1964 following the unexpected heart-attack death of my partner, Bill Grauer. I had not really realized the extent to which he indulged in what I guess we would today call creative financing, creative bookkeeping. It was a big mess, and it went under. After kicking around and not really being put to much use, the Riverside masters were acquired by Fantasy.

After a little bit of back and forth, Fantasy asked me if I would be interested in relocating to San Francisco to run the jazz program that they were then developing – not only the stuff that they had acquired, which was to be extensively reissued, but they were also getting newly involved with a number of artists. It was one of those offers you can't refuse. I came here by myself. I had a wife, Lucy, and two children.

Orrin Keepnews

My younger son was entering his last year in high school, and my wife decided not to dislocate him at that point.

So there I am, a thorough New Yorker, in California, working for a company in Berkeley that involved a couple of people who I knew only slightly. Ralph Kaffel, who became the head of the record company when Saul Zaentz shifted over to his new career as a major movie producer, had been in the wholesale record distribution business in Los Angeles prior to becoming involved with Fantasy. He had been the head of the company that had distributed Riverside. We soon discovered that he and I were probably the only two people in the world who referred to Riverside albums not by their artist names or by their titles, but by their catalog numbers. It wasn't *Cannonball Adderley in San Francisco*; it was 311. He and I knew that! It was a nice, *haimish* [homey] way to start off my life away from home. I found myself a place to temporarily live in Berkeley, but the thing that I wanted to do was drive over the bridge and see what was happening.

I soon discovered this brand-new jazz club in San Francisco, Keystone Korner, which had only been in operation for a few months. But from the marquee [at Keystone Korner, I knew] this was where the music I was looking for would be found. I was curious at the name because it obviously was named cute: each word started with a *K*. I discovered that [Todd Barkan] had taken over the club with that name attached to it. That's been a name that you now associate with an adventurous jazz policy.

I guess that [Keystone] was my first thought of a home. I was very much by myself and trying to find out what the area was all about. I just thought it was a damn good idea to have a natural habitat, so I kind of took up semi-permanent residence, as it were, at Keystone. Todd and I became rather friendly to begin with.

I remember Keystone Korner in these early days, and, you must remember, I come from New York; I am a jazz person. At that point, I had pretty much lived for fifteen or twenty years in jazz clubs. One of the big distinctions between me and other jazz record producers is that I never saw any of my colleagues in the jazz clubs in New York – or damn few of them, anyhow. I had been broken in when I was still in my teens and, for various reasons, used to hang out in New York at the Village Vanguard, so the first club owner I ever got to know was Max Gordon.

Todd will forgive me – or if he won't, tough – but he ain't never been no Max Gordon. The Vanguard is the most extreme example of the success of treating everybody good. And, no, the Vanguard is not perfect, and Lorraine Gordon [who took over after her husband, Max, died] is far from perfect, but that is probably the prototype and probably the reason why the club has been in existence since the '30s. It was a fully functioning folk and cabaret club when I first started going there, which was probably about 1940 when I was seventeen years old. I remember once when Max Gordon had asked my opinion [about the club's musical focus] and I told him, "Don't be ridiculous – stick with what you've got. Don't be so foolish as to put in a jazz policy." And over the years, I would remind him, "Aren't you glad you didn't pay any attention to me?" *I* am! The Vanguard has had a full-time jazz policy since 1955. The point is that the Vanguard really is the prototype.

I've always had good feelings about San Francisco as a jazz town for one extremely personal reason: long before Todd, the city had a couple of strong, eventually legendary jazz clubs. One in particular, in North Beach, was the Jazz Workshop. In 1959, I had done a live-in-the-club recording with the newly formed Cannonball Adderley Quintet for Riverside, and it was the first hit record of my life [*Cannonball Adderley Quintet in San Francisco*]. It owed a lot of its success to the Bobby Timmons 6/8 blues waltz, a catchy song titled "This Here," which opened the album. It was an eleven-minute track preceded by a minute and a half of talk – Cannonball introducing and explaining the song. This was Bobby's second hit tune; a year or so earlier, while with Art Blakey's Jazz Messengers, he had written "Moanin'." So I was aware from the night that I worked in that club that the San Francisco jazz audience was very alert and aware and, under the right circumstances, enthusiastic. When I came out here a dozen years later, that still seemed to be true.

Todd, in that sense, was one of the people [responsible for that awareness and enthusiasm]. He didn't act like a club owner. I don't know if he didn't care to or didn't know how, but he was more like a kid in a candy shop. And I don't know what it was like for an average customer, but I was a professional in this business; I knew most of the people I was going to hear and always felt that I was at least partially at work when I was in a jazz club listening. On the one hand, it was nice that there wasn't any built-in tension in the place; on the other hand, it pretty much drove me crazy how un-businesslike Todd's approach was. As long as it wasn't my problem, it was a lovely way for a jazz club to be.

People would tolerate and do benefits for Todd Barkan because of who he wasn't. He wasn't [like] any other club owner in town that you want to name. I'm not going to go on tape defaming a *particular* club owner, but I'll say he was unlike any other club owner in the town at that time. Todd was perceived of as being well meaning, honest, forthright, and truthful. Not all these things are necessarily accurate, but that's the way he was perceived.

There was a positive attitude on the part of musicians toward him, and musicians are perfectly right to be primarily antagonistic in their attitude toward and their memories of club owners. When there are exceptions, they usually are accurate exceptions – but not necessarily. The musicians are happy to be able to find a club owner that you can say something nice about. And, sometimes, they exaggerate. But by and large, if you're going to compare Todd Barkan with the general run of jazz club owners, you're going to come up with somebody who, while he may not necessarily be the brightest or most admirable character in the world, is still way ahead of average in his class.

Basically, you have two choices if you're running a club: you can attempt to accurately reflect what's out there – what's happening stylistically – or you can use your position as hard as you can to hire people who play the kind of music you like to hear. Todd always struck me as not having too much of a problem that way because he was pretty eclectic himself. He wasn't doing very much in the way of forcing. He was hiring players that he was not unhappy with and he generally was working with a cross-section of what was available. Now, whether this was because musical styles didn't mean very much to him or whether he was legitimately a champion of eclecticism, I don't know, and never felt I did know. I saw him a lot; I got to know him fairly well; but I have to say that what I knew of him didn't necessarily cut very deep. I was not prepared to be his analyst.

I recorded there [at Keystone Korner] a few times. There's a McCoy Tyner album [*Atlantis*] that was done right after Monterey in '74. I recorded Sonny Rollins there and several other people at the club. I was never in the business of buying tapes from anybody else; if I wanted to record a particular act, I was going to record it. If an act of mine was recorded at a club, it would be my recording. I would have no reason to be interested in a recording that had gone on under somebody else's supervision or somebody else's engineer. It just wouldn't have come up. And that has nothing to do, one way or the other, with Todd or the club. I just never would work that way.

It was not the most convenient place to record, the physical setup being what it was, where you've got a rather small stage and a backstage area that wasn't designed to be any kind of control room. We were most apt to hire a recording truck: they'd park on the street, and cables would run into the club from it.

During that time period, you had always at least one other major jazz club in town: the Great American Music Hall was really thriving as a jazz operation. And I remember an occasion when Todd got ambitious. Todd actually had Weather Report booked into the Keystone Korner – indicating that his taste would go that far with a currently hot group – but he also ended up presenting an act [that same week] at the Music Hall. He brought in, and he paid for, Bill Evans. Bill Evans did not draw well at the Great American Music Hall. I was among the not-too-many people who were at the Music Hall practically every night that week. Whether [the Great American Music Hall] didn't have the money or didn't want to spend the money, [Barkan] had the opportunity to put Bill in, and was able to do it. But this was at his cost, and he lost money on it. The last full week that Bill Evans ever played anywhere was at Keystone.

At the end of the week, Weather Report left San Francisco. At that point, their bass player was Miroslav Vitous, and whoever was Todd's girlfriend at the time left town with Miroslav. I remember simply that Todd had the ultimate bad week: he lost money on a club booking, and he lost his old lady to the bass player from the other band.

Courtesy of George Cables and Helen Wray

Keystone Korner

Presents

Showtimes: 8:30 & 10:30 (plus 12:30 Fri & S
Adm $7.50 (Late show $5 except Fri & Sat)

♪Food Service ♪All Ages Welcome ♪Full Bar

Mar 22 - Apr 3:	**WOODY SHAW** Quintet w/ **BOBBY HUTCHERSON** Steve Turre, Mulgrew Miller, Stafford James, Tony Reedu
Apr 7-10:	**JIMMY SMITH** w/ Phil Upchurch
Apr 12-17:	**RED GARLAND & CLIFFORD JORDAN** Quartet
Apr 19-24:	**DAVE LIEBMAN & RICHIE BEIRACH** Quartet Frank Tusa, Ed Moore
Apr 26 - May 1:	**BRUCE FORMAN** Trio PLUS! **JOE FARRELL** feat: Eddie Marshall, Jeff Carney
May 3-8:	**PHIL WOODS** Quartet, w/ **HAL GALPER, BILL GOODWIN, STEVE GILMORE**
May 10-15:	**LOCKJAW DAVIS & SWEETS EDISON**
May 17-22:	**JAKI BYARD & ERIC KLOSS** Quartet
May 24-29:	**FLORA PURIM & AIRTO**
May 31 - June 5:	**ALIVE!**
June 7-12:	**TITO PUENTE** & Latin Percussion Ensemble
June 14-19:	**PAQUITO D'RIVERA** w/HILTON RUIZ
June 21-26:	**SPHERE·CHARLIE ROUSE, BEN RILEY, BUSTER WILLIAMS, KENNY BARRON**

Advance tickets at all BASS outlets (835-3849). Charge tix by phone: 835-4342. Box office opens at noon daily, 6pm weekends. Doors open 8pm. Keystone Kards--ten admissions for $50--always available at the club. Shows produced by Todd Barkan, coordinated by April Magnusson & Mike LeMole. Poster by Tom Copi.

In Order to keep Keystone Korner going, we must not take great music for granted. Your consistent support is necessary for our continued survival. Your attendance even once a month would be wonderful and would make a big difference.

THANK YOU TO ALL THE MUSICIANS, FANS & FRIENDS WHO HAVE MADE OUR CONTINUED SURVIVAL POSSIBLE. BRIGHTER MOMENTS.

Todd C Barkan

One drink minimum per set.   Keystone Hotline: 781-0697.

750 Vallejo, San Francisco

*Courtesy of
George Cables
and Helen Wray*

> **You never went to work when you were at Keystone. You went to play.**
>
> *Carl Burnett*

George Cables

There were nights – I mean, *memorable* nights – with Bobby [Hutcherson] and Eddie Henderson's in the audience being Eddie, making comments on this and that. Everybody would come through there, whether they were playing or not, because it was such a great vibe. You knew you're going to hear some music when you went to Keystone Korner. You going to hear some *music!* Wasn't about half-steppin'.

And Jessica Williams, I remember her first moment there. She walked in [and asked someone] – I think she might even have asked me – "Where's Todd?" or "Where's the owner?" She went in the backroom, which is the office, and emerged maybe ten minutes later, stepped on the stage, which was raised, and started playing solo piano. And she just started playing solo piano on the breaks [between other musicians' sets].

I remember Professor Irwin Corey even opening up for Bobby Hutcherson. He was on the stage: blah blah blah – ya know, talking. But he wouldn't stop! He kept on going. Bobby went up onstage, just stood there – and [Corey's] not stopping. So [Bobby] had to go over to him and physically, gently, move him off the stage, 'cause we needed to play the gig.

Dave Liebman

Mostly, you have to really talk about Miles, 'cause Miles didn't play clubs, not during my time with him in '73, '74. He only played the Keystone and a place called Paul's Mall, which is part of a club called the Jazz Workshop in Boston. Miles by then was a big act and we played concerts; we never played clubs. But he played the Keystone at least once, if not twice. That's a big thing when you have a guy of that magnitude in a small venue where you can see him and really feel him. At least one of the weeks, we had three guitars, not just the normal two.

"Let's turn it up not just to eleven; let's turn it up to eighty." It was a wild week because it was just so loud. I'll never forget it. But Miles enjoyed playing there. And Todd treated him well. That spoke legions about the place because Miles didn't need to play clubs at that time.

Calvin Keys

I saw Miles at Keystone Korner. I was in a line, waiting to go in. As I came up, several women were standing in line – I'll never forget that night – and this girl said, "Oh, yeah, we're going to see Miles. I wonder what kind of music he's going to be doing?" "Well," the other one said, "I just came to see what he's wearing."

Helen Wray

It was *magic* because of the music and the people around it and the musicians. It wasn't the management; it was the people who played there. It was all this fleeting magic that wasn't going to be happening again. That's why it made you feel like you were experiencing something special, that it was just of the moment and you may never hear that again.

Al Young

I remember one night trying to get in to see baritone saxophone player Nick Brignola. He had worked previously with the trumpet player, the Mingus alumnus, Ted Curson, and I had first seen him at Monterey.

This particular night, both Ted and I were out in the lobby trying to get in, and there was a long line. Ted was working and I was there with Luciano Federighi, my Italian translator, who is also a musician and a music writer, and his wife. I thought I could pull rank and get in, but they were being very nasty. These were the late days – we're up to the '80s, now – and Ted was in front of me trying to get in, and I didn't know what was holding him up. But he was in some kind of an argument with the person at the door. So I said, "Hey, how's Nick Brignola?" Ted went off on me. He said, "Nick Brignola – I get so tired of hearing about Nick Brignola." "But," I said, "he's wonderful. I heard him with your band." "Yeah, I know, I know. I brought him in. And now everybody wants to hear about him. Excuse me, man; I'm just an Afro-American jazz musician trying to get into a jazz club to play his own gig. I'm going back to Europe."

Helen Wray	Bill Cosby used to come in occasionally, too. One night, there was a young woman who wanted to come in, and he was standing there by the door. She didn't have the admission money, so he paid for her ticket. Keystone brought that out in people. A real shared experience.
devorah major	When Ornette [Coleman] came, it was a very small house – fifty, seventy-five people. Intermission comes, and almost everybody leaves; there's half a dozen people left in the club. So we go backstage, and he's just as sweet, as warm . . . and we're talking, and he says, "Are you girls out of college?" and I said, "No, I'm still in college." He says, "That's great. This is why jazz is gonna stay alive." And we said, "Thank you," and he said, "So were you planning on staying for the second set?" and we said, "Is there gonna be a second set?" And he said, "Well, if you're stayin', there's a second set. We'll play for you." We got a second set of Ornette Coleman. He was paid to play for the night; he loved to play music; and he had three young women who loved to listen. Those are the kinds of things that happened.
George Cables	*Listening* to music was so great. I can remember seeing McCoy playing and I could swear the piano was being levitated, was going up and going all over as the music was being played. The kind of energy that he generated, the music . . . Oh, it was great.
Steve Turre	I remember one time Walid, who worked the door, we went fishing on a boat out of Fisherman's Wharf. I caught a great big old salmon, maybe three feet long. We put it in the beer freezer at Keystone until the gig was over. Then, the next day, I invited the band out to my folks' and we all barbequed that sucker. Had a big feast.
Ronnie Matthews	One summer when I was at Diablo Valley College doing the Jamey Aebersold clinic, somebody canceled out on Todd and he called me; [he also] got James Leary and Joe Henderson, maybe Woody [Shaw]. There were a whole bunch of us that were in the area, so he pulled us in there to fill in for two or three nights. And the musicians were all on a very high level, so it was wonderful to walk into that. That's

something – that Todd would be able to pull all these guys together totally spontaneously.

Ora Harris

When Art Blakey brought Wynton Marsalis to the Keystone Korner, that was a real big deal. No one knew who he was; they just knew he had this suit and this tie and it made him look good, and he just played so well and people were just screaming and hollering. That was another thing about the Keystone Korner. The audience was so free to express themselves with the musicians and it made such joy.

Helen Wray

I remember when Wynton first came out to Keystone to play with Art, and he had heard that I was studying classical flute. After the gig one night, he sat down and played Vivaldi, a movement from the Vivaldi trumpet concerto, just for me. It was so lovely and so beautiful. I felt so honored. They did things like that. You had that personal relationship; something to do with the place induced that.

Bob Stewart

We happened to be playing opposite Horace Silver. Our group had tuba and cello and guitar and drums and alto, and every set, Horace Silver honored us by coming up and standing at the end of the bar over by the door, the entryway, and watching us play. I was like, "Well I'll be damned!" I mean, he stayed there the whole set – the whole three or four days we were there – to stand at the bar and listen to what this group was doing. I was so honored. It was an amazing week for me.

devorah major

Music informs writing, and Keystone *so* informed my writing. Often, I would go to Keystone Korner and I would come home and I'd be buzzing – literally, my skin would be buzzing – and I would sit and write. I owned a little Olivetti typewriter that had a corrective ribbon, but mostly I composed by hand and I would either journal or write poems. They might have been about the Black Power struggle or about freedom; the music made me free, so I wrote [about] freedom rather than writing per se about music. It opened me to catch what I needed to catch. And so Keystone certainly fed my poetry, but not in terms of being poetry about music.

I have a poem I wrote called "The Day after the April 9th Evening Blues," April 9 being my birthday. It really is a very sad love poem. I was just totally in love with this guy. He was older and he was just playing me, and I had my birthday and he hadn't even called. But I went to Keystone for my birthday. And then I wrote "The Day after." I named it as blues, but it wasn't structured as a blues; I was singin' the blues.

Helen Wray

George [Cables] played for me a lot. I think it was after Keystone closed, when he moved in with me, that he wrote "Helen's Song" and a lullaby he wrote for me. Now, my whole family has songs. My sisters have songs; my mother has a song called "Helen's Mother's Song." He recorded them on the solo album he did in New York recently [*You Don't Know Me*]. "Okay, the next one's 'Honeylu'; it's for Lorraine." "Okay, the next one is 'Stickarella,'" that's my other sister. The producer of the album said, "God, are there any more sisters? We're going to be here all night." I have four, so we all have songs. The previous dog has a song; [George's] mother and father have songs too.

BRIGHT MOMENTS!

Cecil Taylor Woodblock by Kristen Wetterhahn

Announcing

the Keystone Gallery

Come and Celebrate Our Opening   Showing Visions of Jazz   Photography • Graphics • Painting

Current Exhibit: Tom Copi, Bruce Polonsky, Wanda Lucente, Kathy Sloane, Jerry Stoll, Flicka McGurrin, Angela Beske, Don Broder, Bryan McMillen, Ronald Ragland, Kristen Wetterhahn.

Thursday, April 23 :: 4-7 p.m.

Gallery Hours: 7:30 p.m. - 1:00 a.m. Nightly   *Wine & Cheese Served.*

Tom Copi.   Kristen Wetterhahn   *Curating*

IN COORDINATION WITH TODD BARKAN   **KEYSTONE KORNER, 750 Vallejo, North Beach, SF**

Courtesy of George Cables and Helen Wray

Cecil Taylor, 1977

Anthony Braxton, 1978

Muhal Richard Abrams, 1979

David "Fathead" Newman, 1979

I was inspired by Monk because quintessentially he was like a poet writing in notes, in musical notes. *Jack Hirschman*

Jack Hirschman

I didn't have any dough to go to Keystone. I absolutely did not. None at all. I was here in '73, '74, but if [friends of mine] mentioned Keystone Korner, I would say, "Well, I'm sorry, but I don't have . . ." – what was it, six or seven bucks to go in? I just didn't have that money. But I was very lucky that [a few years later], my girl [Kristen Wetterhahn] worked at Keystone Korner. I'm talking about the period 1977 or '78, because I knew Keystone from that period to '83, when it closed. Kristen got the job at Keystone and, like I say, I was pleased because I love jazz. And as it turned out, in that period my son, David, was down in Santa Cruz, and he was broadcasting jazz on the Santa Cruz station. Jazz was very much a part of our life.

Because of our jobs, we were really night people. We wouldn't eat supper, Kristen and I, 'til 2:30 in the morning. So what would happen is, I would come out of our apartment on Kearny Street [and go] to Spec's Café, which is where I was drinking and reading poetry; I'd be with the poets, or the folks, workers, and we'd be reading poetry, yabbering. At about a quarter to twelve [at night], I'd walk down to Coit Liquors, before they closed, and get a bottle of wine for our dinner. And then I'd walk over to Keystone, and because Kristen was working there, I was able to get in free. This was an incredible gift indeed because here were some of the great jazz musicians of the time, and I was able to hear them.

Keystone had a very big part for me in that period from '77 to '83. I used to do these Russian-American posters and give them away. They were really communist; they were communist propaganda. It was sort of like my daily jazz, and they were done almost entirely in a crazy, improvising state. I did between about thirty and fifty a day in the apartment that we lived in, and there was a big influence of the jazz world on that.

Jack Hirschman

I would take a piece of paper, let's say eight-by-eleven – although I must tell you that I would use all kinds of papers that I would find in the dumpsters, and some beautiful cardboards and all – and I would make several gestures on the paper. The first gesture would be sort of a graphic gesture; it could be out of Zen or something oriental. Then, I would write a Russian word, like *Iskra*, the name of the revolutionary newspaper, which means "spark." And on top of the word "spark," in Russian Cyrillic, I would write "ameruss," a word I made up – a combination from America and Russia, a pun on *amorous*. And then, underneath it, I would write "communist" in Cyrillic. Then I would write on the side of the paper, "a solidarity." It could be a solidarity Haiti, or it could be a solidarity ULW, which is the Union of Left Writers. And then, underneath, I would say something like, "no class." On the other side of the paper: "no Klan" or "no Nazis" or "no nukes." It would be like a slogan.

And then, there would be a *presenté*, someone who was a revolutionary figure like Che, or Lenin, or poets, using also a lot of jazz, you know. Like it would be Charlie Parker *presenté*, or one of the other jazz guys who no longer was with us, but *was* with us. It could be anyone in that realm. And then I would write a little poem, like a haiku poem, just a very short improvisation. I gave many, many thousands to the people coming to the club [Keystone Korner].

I was inspired by Monk because quintessentially he was like a poet writing in notes, in musical notes. The most fecund evening I ever had in my poetic life was one evening [when] I was going through a break with my first wife. I was down in a place in Echo Park [in Los Angeles], I put on a Monk record, and I wrote that night eighty-one what I call "rifficals," jazz improvisations using whatever arsenal I had – which goes back to James Joyce as well as what was opened up by jazz. But these are actually jazz poems. There is another poem that I wrote called "Schnapps' Son," which is also inspired by Monk. [Charlie] Parker's really involved in it. And it's a poem that's been published, and some of the rifficals have been, too. I was literally inspired by listening to "Blue Monk" on the disk [LP]. He was very close to me, just as someone who uses words. It's like he is using words because he is speaking in notes, more than, I believe, any other pianist that I've ever heard. Cecil Taylor, who also is a writing poet, fills the plane up and all [the] spaces, while Monk is made of breaths. He's closer to some of the things that were going on in American writing from Charles Olson – the use of breath on the line and all. That's very close to things that Monk [was] involved in.

Post–World War [II], jazz, abstract expressionism, and what I call field composition in poetry represent for me the trinity of essential American idioms that really are the foundation of not merely my work, but the work of virtually a whole generation of writers and musicians. What Parker enunciated. What Jackson Pollock enunciated. Jackson Pollock really did break open the world of art and made New York the center – not Paris any longer – but it was the idiom, [although] not merely the idiom of dripping. What Jackson did, and in a certain sense Parker did the same thing in music, was completely revolutionize the line. The line, l-i-n-e, the line was revolutionized by him in terms of what he did. And that line, the revolution was so deep, that literally today, we're talking 2006, in the hotels around this place, people are lifting up brushes and doing it, resonating to the incredible shift of line that Jackson created in the '40s and early '50s.

Once [at Keystone], we were talking and someone – it was Dexter, or it may have been Dewey Redman – was talking about Charlie Parker: what was the nature of his genius? He said that musicians in those days, even in '81, '82, could not fully understand how Parker did it. It was such a rapid grooving the way he slid, not just in tempo, from one level of the music to the other. Still to that day, people were incapable of doing it. That was one of the real essences of his genius – that he was able to move through the jazz dimensions of a particular piece with an incredible grooved rapidity.

The African American dimension has been a major influence on virtually all the artists in this country, even if people don't want to admit it. It is the basis, the musical basis, at the level of popular creation. Jazz is the musical foundation of our contemporary lives. I don't mean simply that it is part of everyone's life in America, but it's a part within ourselves. I know, for example, as a creator, as a poet, that all I have to do is tap into something in myself, something that I do with my own breath, that opens me to the African American dimension and therefrom unfolds words or sounds or even paint. So it's a very important part. Why shouldn't it be? Because this, politically speaking, is a country which has always claimed itself to be democratic, but we know that that was bullshit. There was, in fact, slavery in the country. If you have slavery in a whole portion of the country, you're not a democratic country. And the liberation of that slavery is, creatively speaking, the most important thing that probably has occurred in the American last century. And it's understood that way in other countries. In other words, if you go to Europe, Europe understands that. Jazz is the language of a liberation into democracy.

The Russians were very hip to early American jazz modes. I remember translating [Vladimir] Mayakovsky with a friend one day, and he came upon a word, *ki-ka-poo.* And he didn't know what it was in Russian. And I didn't know what it was in American. And three days later, he checked it and said, "Well, you know, there was a dance in 1915 from America called the kickapoo, named after the Kickapoo Indians." But it was a jazz dance, like a foxtrot or something. An American jazz dance tune! Just a little craze that went on.

When you speak of the thumping in hip-hop, that, of course, has certain relations to the old jazz thing, but it also has to do with the [Russian] revolution. A lot of hip-hoppers don't even know this. But someone like Mayakovsky, the Russian poet, was writing in those internal rhymes on the street level at the beginning of the twentieth century. And the drum – he even has a line, "Speed is our god, drum pumped aorta." And in a certain sense, if you listen to him poppin', the rapidity and the drum, it's all there, too. So there were always bases of things.

Put it this way. In nineteenth-century European music and in America, you had the translation into what we call "light music" – theater, you know, dance, etc. But that was intercepted toward the end of the century by the music that came out of the liberation from slavery. And when you get into the twentieth century, when you get to Scott Joplin and all, and you get toward the foundations of jazz, you have a language that comes from the struggle of liberation. It has pervaded the entire twentieth century right up even to now [in the twenty-first century].

I was born in the United States. I'm not a European. I was born in New York in '36. I worked for four years as a copy boy for the Associated Press, on Fifty-First Street. On Fifty-Second Street, Charlie Parker was playing when I was working and I didn't go. I could kick myself for this. I was just a young novice and I wanted to be, first, a reporter and then a novelist, a poet. I knew almost after the fact of that gang: Charlie and Miles playing on Fifty-Second Street. It was literally around the corner....

I came to southern California in '61 and moved to San Francisco in late '72, and then Kristen and I met in late '74. We lived here in North Beach and Keystone became part of our life [starting] from about '77 or '78. You remember that time, after the Vietnam War, before the Sandinistas in '79. I had already started to work with the Sandinista cultural group before the overthrow of Somoza. And then in '80, Reagan came into power and he pulled that number with the air controllers, and then there was a lot of consolidation of the Left against him. [The year] '82, of course, was very significant 'cause my jazz-broadcasting son [David] had contracted leukemia, which developed into lymphoma, and he passed away in 1982. And at the time Keystone was folding, Kristen and I sort of folded. In fact, it was pretty synchronous.

There was also in '82 a big conference of writers, the Left/Right Conference, and Todd Barkan was very generous with me in organizing particular events at Keystone Korner. We had political poetry readings, and they weren't merely readings on a particular Sunday; we would [sometimes] have political events there before the place opened in the evening. I believe there was one against Reagan. Amiri Baraka came out; I read with Amiri. I mean, he was really the headlining poet, but I was the local one. And then, later on, we became really good friends. Last year, we had a marvelous time together in Naples where we read for my Italian publisher.

That Keystone opened itself to political events was very important because by that time the prices had gone up to seven, eight, maybe ten bucks, and here what you had were events in which people could hear something politically involved and, if they gave a bit of bread, it was really going to go to the cause. It wasn't so much going to Keystone; Keystone just wanted the bar [income], which was perfectly fine.

It was a heady place on one level. In fact, given that the cop station was next door, it was screwbally. I never understood it. Around the music world, there was lots of drinking [and] dopiness. But there were wonderful occasions.

Keystone became something very personal apart from the personal sense that I was living with Kristen and she was working there. On a sadder note: I mentioned my son, David, who died of lymphoma in 1982 in his home in Venice, [California]. He was twenty-five, so he was quite young but very involved in the jazz world. It wasn't simply that he loved jazz; he was also a photographer of jazz. He did some wonderful, wonderful photographs of jazz musicians, and after he died, I exhibited the stuff that he did at a couple of local exhibitions. When he died, I wrote an arcane, one of my longer poems, an elegy for David, called "The David Arcane," and it was published in a little edition, and the picture he took of Bobby Hutcherson playing at Keystone was used as the frontispiece of the book.

Woodcut of Sonny Stitt   by Kristen Wetterhahn

SONNY STITT

Played just about to the very end,
Played good the reed, disciplined the groove.

Ankle unchained excelsior gut-bellow
spiral breath in the cheekbones

still circulating with distinguished
flecks in disk heaven.
— Jack Hirschman
Homage to Sonny Stitt from Todd Barkan and Keystone Korner 1982

*Courtesy of George Cables
and Helen Wray*

Carla Bley, 1979

We were all thin.
We all had more hair.

George Cables

Helen Wray

Today, there are many wonderful, young musicians. They're extraordinary. It's wonderful they're keeping that music going. But they're emulating these people that have already done that. Maybe it's just because I'm getting older [that] I don't hear it as strongly in the present generation, as wonderful as they are.

I think the generation of musicians of Dexter's era definitely had it harder than the kids coming out of Juilliard and music schools today. There was something about the music at that time, when all those guys were still here – I don't know what it is. My only thought is they did have it harder, having lived under segregation when they were traveling. We all got closest to the African American bands. They seemed to be the warmest, if you can generalize. I probably shouldn't generalize because it wasn't across the board like that.

I hear George [Cables] talk about when he was a young musician coming up and he was on the road with Joe Henderson and how hard it was. They had to pay their own accommodations, and Joe didn't pay the guys very much. So they'd bunk two in a room and they'd barely have enough money to eat. And the drugs were so prevalent in the clubs then; it was hard to avoid it. Luckily, the young guys today aren't into all the coke and stuff that was going around then.

Stuart Kremsky

Jazz is even more marginal than it was at the time [of Keystone Korner]. There's no longer a circuit of West Coast clubs. At the time, you could book people up and down the West Coast, and you could actually make it viable. Or very often, they'd be stopping on the way to or from Japan; that would be a common kind of scheduling. But the clubs aren't there any more. I think [the change had to do with] a lot of factors all combining. A lot of the older, well-known names are now dead or retired, or whatever. Newer names aren't as big a draw. It's also changed from a club music to a concert music. I don't know if that's a good thing necessarily, but where [you] used to have a club scene, now you have a concert circuit and a festival circuit. So, instead of playing clubs for a [full] week, you'll do a lot of one-night stands and festivals. I imagine musicians don't like it as much. Maybe they go out for less time, but they have to travel so much more. When you play for a week in a town, you have a chance to settle in, but on the other hand, you'd be away from home for that much longer. The scene's different. It's hard to say if the clubs closed and then that changed the scene, or if the scene changed and that closed the clubs, but it's just not what it used to be. It's not necessarily better or worse; it's just different.

Carl Burnett

When people started playing concerts instead of clubs, that changed everything. That changed the way all the jazz clubs were run. [Clubs] made their money from you being there for a week. When the concerts started, what you made playing [in clubs] for a week, you [now] made in a night. But then you started doing it for the money and sacrificed the love and the cycle that the people fed, because you were too far away from them. You never felt them no more. People showed their appreciation, but the appreciation was different. Even though they all applauded and said they liked it, there was a disconnect that took place [in the concert halls].

In Keystone, you could see everybody and everybody could see you. When people left there, you didn't know if you'd ever see them again – but nine chances out of ten, they might be back the next night. You'd see them again.

Jack Hirschman

Those were the days in North Beach [when] you always knew there'd be the line outside Keystone to get into the early show, and even the late shows. And those were the days when North Beach filled with people coming from all over, not merely to go to Keystone, because Keystone held like 220 people, I think. There were other venues that were very active before Reagan; I'm talking about before '80 when the boom came down [from] the landlords. And so there were a lot of venues, poetry venues. And people were coming from all over the city and the Bay Area. And on Union Street, there was Intersection, which had poetry readings virtually five, six nights a week. The streets were full; they were full of the . . . I shouldn't say vestigial bones, because I don't think it's simply a vestigial bone (American street madness) because it's always embodied that. But the streets were filled with a lot of people.

The energy is different now. This place we're sitting at [Caffe Trieste] is one of the energy high points, and, on certain evenings, Spec's is another high point. Vesuvio's – there's still a bit of energy down there. But there was a creative energy [during the Keystone years]. There was much more creative energy.

Ronnie Matthews

You don't have clubs like that any more, with a house rhythm section, and [you] can bring in people to play with them and not really lose anything in terms of the performance because the musicians are on such a high level. See, that, too, is kind of unique. It's always best to have a group that works together all the time; I don't think anything can really beat that. But if you have a rhythm section like that [at Keystone], it's not going to be exactly like a working group but it's not going to be bad. You won't feel sorry that you came there to see it.

Steve Turre

The quality of the music that Keystone brought in always had a certain level of artistic integrity – of artistic quality and creative meaning. And then I look at what some of the premier jazz clubs in the Bay Area are bringing in today: it's not always about the quality or the artistry; it's just about whatever they think is going to sell. And I know people have to stay in business, but there's a way to do it. I don't think Keystone closed because the music wasn't bringing in the dollars. I think it was just a matter of some unfortunate business decisions and circumstances that brought the house down. . . . There's a way to build a house of integrity and have it stand and not succumb to mediocrity, which is the norm here in America today.

Eddie Henderson

When the Keystone closed, the bottom dropped out. There are many good players here, but I'm talking about the real deal, the heroes. It's not cost effective to come [to the Bay Area] because there's no venues here any more. They can't come to [Jazz at] Pearl's 'cause Pearl's can't afford 'em. And come to Yoshi's? It's not the same as the Keystone Korner; just look at the lineup of people that they hire. It's not a *jazz* club. I don't know how to put it. It's a little clique. You have to be the right young lion, or the right age, or white-ish, or . . .

George Cables

That's one place I never got bored on the breaks. These days, when you take a break, you start looking at your watch. I used to be good for hanging at the bar, but I don't do that any more. I kind of get quiet, get a space. You're there to play music and you're lookin' around, and occasionally you see that there are people you can hang out with or that you want to spend time with. But it's not quite the same, not the same spirit [as Keystone]. In those days, it was very easy to not just see your *old* friends but make new friends as well.

Carl Burnett

It was unique to play with the Three Sounds. When I joined the band, every place the Three Sounds played, [the bassist] Andy Simpkins and his wife took names of people. And they communicated with those people. Every time we got ready to go back there, they'd send letters and let them know we were coming. And every place we played was a sold-out house, even though we never had a hit record. But it was all friends. And that's what Keystone was. It was like all friends.

Dave Liebman

I always enjoyed coming here [to Keystone]. And, of course, the main thing was that you could play what you wanted to, and Todd Barkan was completely cool and even joined in. He's on one of my records playing percussion. He was a musician, he was savvy, he knew what was going on, but he ran a real club.

Of course, there was the atmosphere of the times. Very loose, big hang. You were there late, real late, listening to music. Checking out Dexter Gordon. It was the jazz life. Todd tried to recreate that, no question about it. He tried to have that vibe of what it must have been like, I guess, in the '50s and '60s. By the '70s, this was getting more and more uncommon, even in New York. Jazz was changing. The music was changing. The audience was changing. Fusion was coming in. It was going to big halls. The main groups played big places. And so the whole idea of a club where you played three sets and the last set was basically musicians and artists [in the audience], that was already starting to go by the mid-'70s, certainly by the late '70s. And the way the economy went, the expenses of keeping a club and running a place [were escalating]. So this was one of the last of the Mohicans.

David Williams

The whole music business was totally different at that time. It was a period that was all about the music, nothing but the music. Now, it's about business. A lot of the younger musicians now are so much more business-minded. Maybe this is the right way; I don't know. There was so much we robbed ourselves of. We were exploited so much more than the younger musicians are now. But that was then.

Todd Barkan

If I had my most passionate druthers, I would wish that place would still be open. Because it would be a hell of a statement at this point to have anything like that open in the world.

Donald Rafael Garrett, Craig Harris, 1981

Archie Shepp, 1980

Dannie Richmond, 1981

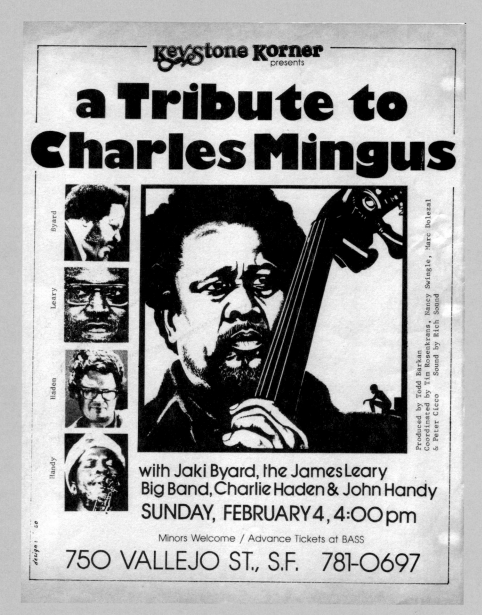

Courtesy of George Cables and Helen Wray

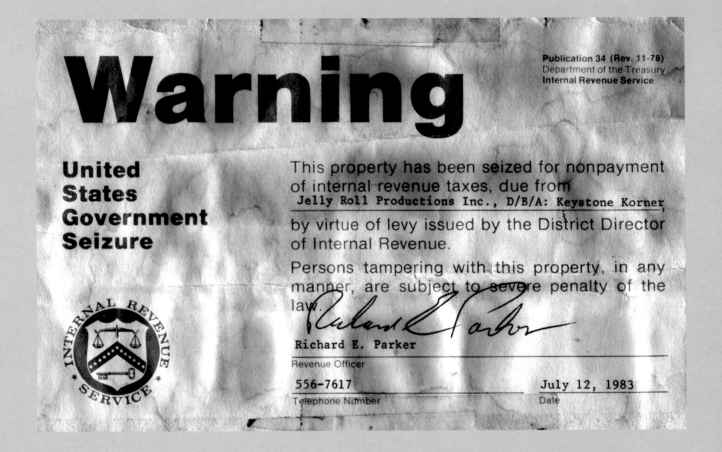

July 12, 1983
Courtesy of George Cables and Helen Wray

> A gauntlet has been thrown down
> for generations as a way that the
> music can be presented.
>
> *Todd Barkan*

Todd Barkan

Well, it always had financial problems. Keystone closed because of financial problems, but also because I didn't know where to turn in terms of financing it. Yeah, it closed because of financial problems, but as much as anything it closed because of myself: I think I ran out of steam of knowing how to keep it open. My creative adrenaline had run out.

Eddie Marshall

It lasted so long and Todd was so dedicated. You know, a lot of people would've folded that club in two years. I really have a hard time when I hear people try to suggest criminal activity, that his integrity was questionable. I say, "What are you talking about?" I don't hear many musicians talking like that. I don't hear that so much any more, but I certainly heard it – mostly about cocaine. I don't know if they felt that they didn't get their share or had to badmouth him. I don't know.

Stuart Kremsky

As I recall, everybody got paid, but you wouldn't necessarily get paid when you expected it. Sometimes, you would suffer. You had to come on Friday or Saturday night – on the big nights – 'cause that's when the cash would be there and you could get paid.

Eventually, everybody got paid. I think the government got stiffed. I think it was FICA and stuff that made him close, but that was years after I had worked there.

Al Young

In Todd Barkan's mind, Keystone maintained equilibrium; the spirit was the same from the beginning to the last days. But in the public mind, in the jazz audience's mind, Keystone went through disconcerting changes. People were accusing it, in its last days especially, of having become too commercial and too restrictive. It meant that they had people shaking you down at the door; it meant that you couldn't just go in there and pay fifty cents or a dollar or whatever it was and stay all night, that they would put you out after a set. They really started to look at the economy and do practical things. It didn't have that loose "I'm okay, you're okay" feeling that endeared [it to] people in the beginning.

Todd did go through a period there where he was highly unpredictable and no fun to be around. He didn't spin that to the musicians, but mainly to the patrons, the customers. One night, I was sitting by [Gerald Wiggins playing] the piano. Behind the piano was the door to the dressing room. The door was open and a draft was coming in. He said, "Excuse me, man. Could you close the door? There's a draft that's bothering my fingers," and so I said, "Sure," and closed the door. A few minutes later, Todd came out. This was Todd in his late glory days, and he said, "Who closed the door, man?" I said, "I closed the door." He said, "Why did you close the door, Al?" I said, "I closed the door because Gerald Wiggins said it was bothering his fingers." He looked at Gerald, who was in mid-performance and didn't respond, even though I think he was following the conversation. Then Todd said, "You weren't supposed to touch that door, man. Didn't you see the sign on the door?" I said, "No." He said, "I want to show you the sign on the door." So he took me to the door and it had a sign on it: an encircled turkey with a red bar struck through it. He said, "Didn't you see that, man? No turkeys allowed back here. No turkeys can touch the door." I said, "Todd, am I a turkey?" "Yeah, man. I said don't touch the door." He was just impossible.

That particular night, I just had to bite my tongue and let it go, but the piano player thought it was funny. He was amused. And so did [the leader of the group that night] Illinois Jacquet. He just kind of looked around like "Whoa." I'm sure these guys had seen a lot worse than that. That's when strange people were coming into the club. You could tell that something was going on there.

Ronnie Matthews

I remember one very funny incident just before it closed. I was in the club in the afternoon. We were rehearsing or practicing, and this unbelievably beautiful lady came to the door. She was trying to get in; she was looking for Todd. She was really gorgeous, a black lady, and she had a little attaché case or one of those folding leather briefcases. I don't think Todd was even there, but she wanted to see him and whoever was there was saying [to me], "You don't open the door for anybody," and so I couldn't let her in.... But anyway, it turned out – which for me was a real downer – she was from the IRS. Oh man. [Laughs hard] Really brought me down.

Helen Wray

I think we'd known for a couple of months that it was going to be closing. In the end, we were buying all our liquor from Coit and wheeling it up the street, which was quite illegal because we'd lost the liquor license. People weren't coming in, and even the last week wasn't crowded. We just kept it going as long as we could. Then Todd left, and it was just winding down to nothing. I just remember it being sad.

That last night, I walked around, and the managers were taking photos off the wall – all the photos in the backroom that made that backroom. I guess a lot of that stuff was auctioned off, [including] the piano. Eventually, they got rid of everything.

Charles McPherson's band was playing. I suspect he never got paid. We didn't. It didn't seem to matter at the time. I have a feeling George [Cables] might have been there. George has closed a lot of clubs. He closed the Lighthouse in L.A.; he closed Bradley's in New York. The last night was minimal people; we were just serving soft drinks. You knew it was the end of something very special. It just closed so quietly. It was a sad kind of ending. It didn't close with a bang; it just kind of limped out.

Flicka McGurrin

I was working at Keystone Korner for about five years as a cocktail waitress, and I was there when it closed. That was a night I was supposed to work. There was a chain on the door and the [California] State Board of Equalization had taken over the club. They had taken it over a few weeks before and started to take all the cash out of the registers. But I guess they weren't making enough money fast enough and they finally just locked the doors.

I was given $5 that night because there was no work. And I ran into Charles McPherson on the street, who was pounding the pavement, extremely frustrated because his name was on the marquee, but he did not have a job and no place to play. So I said, "Well, I just got my $5. Let me buy you a drink, make you feel better." So we went across the street to Hawaii West and he had a double. And that was the end of Keystone Korner as we knew it, which was really sad.

Eddie Henderson

Keystone was the end of an era in terms of quote-unquote jazz music, culture, in the Bay Area. I know they had Kimball's; they had Kimball's East, Kimball's West. They have Yoshi's. Now, lo and behold, [Yoshi's] is going to open again at Fillmore West. Miles Davis told me one time, "Any time you start getting popular musically, you ain't playing shit." Blue Note, Yoshi's – they're like McDonald's. They don't care about the artists; they just care about economics. Profit and loss. But God bless the Keystone. It was a divine event. . . . Kingdoms rise and fall.

Helen Wray

When I go to New York now and I run into someone who played [at Keystone] and I say, "I'm Helen. I worked at the Keystone," *instantly* there's this connection with the person, because anyone that worked or played there knew what that feeling was at that place. As funky as it was and as smoky as it was, it was conducive to this incredible music that came out of it.

I'm sure there are other places like Keystone in the world, where, at a certain time when certain people come together at a certain place, they make a certain art form happen. It just had all the right ingredients for something special to happen. And you *knew* it was special when you were there, when you were a part of it. I did. It just was that time, and it wouldn't probably happen today. It would never happen like that again. It was of its time.

Orrin Keepnews

The positive vibrations that it gave out toward musicians and toward audiences – that was what worked for it. That was what made it a thriving place and an enjoyable place. What worked against it would seem to have been largely Todd's inability to run an appropriate business organization. And I say that only because there was a while that he was succeeding, as far as anybody could tell. The place looked good, it felt good, and musicians had nice things to say about it. And then, eventually, with no noticeable change in any circumstances, it was gone.

Todd Barkan

We're at Dizzy's Club at Jazz at Lincoln Center about twenty-three years after Keystone Korner in San Francisco closed. Twenty-three years later. And it feels like it's almost historically just a glitch in time because there are times when I'm speaking about what's going on at Dizzy's when I'll think to myself, before I speak, "Oh, and tonight at

Keystone . . ." I haven't yet said it out loud. It's a wonderful thing to feel like your life's work is still continuing, and Keystone Korner was very much a part of my life's work and the life's work of a lot of people who contributed to it.

I was just a far-out hippie like anybody else. I don't know if I had an articulable vision, like Wynton does with this institution [Jazz at Lincoln Center]. Wynton's a profoundly articulate visionary who has stated many times what our mission and purpose are here, in the house of swing. I didn't think of Keystone Korner in such grandiose terms. I was too busy surviving. I knew I wanted the best jazz club I could get and keep it open. It was a labor of love.

It was a very wonderful, wonderful moment in time, and it really points out what the possibilities are of presenting this music. It's a very positive parameter of how much love can be involved in presenting music in a very meaningful way. It's a standard. A gauntlet has been thrown down for generations as a way that the music can be presented. But it takes personal commitment. And you know, it takes a lot of strength to do it. I'm still feeling committed to that effort, the willingness to make that effort.

Orrin Keepnews

Its significance was that it has remained as a legend. Its significance is as a positive image. Its significance is that it reminds a lot of people – when you think about it, or when you bring it up, or when you tell the story again – that, hey, it is possible to put together some positive ingredients and have a good, working jazz club.

Todd Barkan

I have joyful memories tinged with sadness; [I have] a great love of that era and that time and that feeling and that spirit. It is immortalized in recordings, photo collections, things being published, and the memories of all of us who were there. Stuff is scattered; they're scattered to the four winds. It's all over the place as befits a hippie jazz club. Keystone wasn't put away. It was creatively cremated.

Malachi Favors, 1977

Elvin Jones, 1977

Percy Heath,
1979

Buster Williams, 1976

Don Pullen, 1981

Sonny Stitt, 1977

"I like this club."--Miles Davis

"I really feel at home here."--McCoy Tyner

"Best Audience in the world."--Horace Silver

"Greatest Jazz club in the world."--Stan Getz

"My heart belongs to Keystone Korner."--Art Blakey

"The Birdland of the Eighties."--Mary Lou Williams

"It is a great honor every time I play at Keystone Korner."--George Benson

"In no other club in the world can you find the consistent level of musical quality and intensity, dedication, and just plain good feeling that you can find at Keystone Korner."--Max Roach

BILL GRAHAM PRESENTS

A
Benefit
Concert
To Save

Keystone Korner

Featuring:

ERNIE ANDREWS
RICHIE COLE & Alto Madness
JON HENDRICKS
DAVE LIEBMAN & RICHIE BEIRACH
MANHATTAN TRANSFER
BOBBY McFERRIN
D'ALAN MOSS

8pm, Saturday March 19
Warfield Theater
982 Market
San Francisco

This concert is dedicated to the memory of
JACK WHITTEMORE.
He gave as much to this music as anyone ever has.

Courtesy of George Cables and Helen Wray

Horace Silver,
1978

Kathy Sloane
Courtesy of Samuel Wooten

Kathy Sloane

I came to jazz with the significant men in my life. My father had stacks of jazz and classical 78s in those brown multi-disk albums, which he carted with him for his whole life. On some Sunday afternoons, he'd play Benny Goodman or Paul Whiteman on our hi-fi set, though I didn't really listen. More often, he played Bach and Beethoven, which made me feel sad. Paul Robeson's deep, warm, vibrant voice was the sound that I liked the most. My parents were socialists, and Robeson was a particular favorite of theirs. My father never played popular music or blues or Charlie Parker, and I never saw my parents dance, though family lore claimed that my father had once been taken to the Cotton Club and learned to dance from Ella Fitzgerald.

As a kid, I loved words: I read voraciously and enjoyed talking. As a teenager, I listened to *Songs for Young Lovers* and other Sinatra albums, and I danced to '50s pop, but I was not immersed in music of any kind, despite taking three or four years of requisite piano lessons. Perhaps I would have learned more from my father's music had I not been in constant rebellion, but I carried and retained more of his values and the music than I ever admitted.

I first heard live jazz in 1961 on the night I got married, when my young husband, Mickey, took me to hear Mary Lou Williams. I can't recall the name of that bar in midtown Manhattan, but I can remember feeling very grown-up, even though I was just twenty-one. The bartender wanted ID, which I didn't have with me (and Mickey wasn't even twenty-one yet). We explained that we had just gotten married, and the bartender relented, suggesting I light a cigarette so that I would look older in case a bar inspector came in. I choked on the cigarette, but he let us stay. I wasn't sure how to listen to the music.

In 1962, while we were still seniors in college, Mickey took me to hear John Coltrane with McCoy Tyner, Jimmy Garrison, and Elvin Jones at the Half Note on Spring Street in the lower Village, where the bandstand sat above the bar; if you sat at the bar, the musicians were only a few feet away. Many years later, Mickey told me that Elvin had flirted with me from the bandstand all evening, but all I remember is being mesmerized by the man with the horn who appeared to be playing straight up from his belly button! I had never seen or heard a musician whose sound felt so connected to his body, and I didn't have to think about how to listen. The music simply embraced me.

After Mickey and I divorced in 1965, a new boyfriend, Durward, took me to the Five Spot to hear Charles Mingus and Thelonious Monk, and to Slugs in the far East Village. Durward's best friend was Omar Clay, a drummer who backed Sarah Vaughan in those days. Omar knew all the musicians and introduced me to Mingus. The music was strange to me and I think I was both frightened and excited by it. Years later, in 1976, when I met Mingus again backstage at the Berkeley Jazz Festival, he said I looked familiar. I told him I was just another Jewish girl from New York, and that tickled him, so he gave me permission to photograph him right there in his dressing room. He invited me to visit him and his wife, Sue, the next time I came to New York, and I took him up on his offer the following year, bringing prints of the photos to his East Village apartment.

Between 1965 and 1971, with an incomplete M.A. in English from the City University of New York, I taught high school dropouts how to read and college students how to write and read better. And I listened to Aretha Franklin and Otis Redding and the Temptations. Most important during that period, I gave birth to my daughter, Ayisha, who was born in September 1970. Six months later, I joined her father Curtis, a Smokey Robinson and the Miracles kind of guy, in Seattle, and when he and I separated in August 1971 I came down to the Bay Area for a visit and never left. I was a single mother and Berkeley felt like an easier place than New York in which to raise a child alone. I found a job and a place to live, but in the back of my mind I was always going to go back to New York. After several visits back east, however, it became quite apparent that my daughter, a gentle, dreamy child, was miserable in New York, and I acquiesced to remaining in the Bay Area until she went off to college.

My father had been an amateur photographer when I was small, and often, when I woke up late at night for a drink of water or company, he would pick me up and carry me into the kitchen, where the light had become amber and the room smelled of photo-fixer chemicals. He took many pictures of our family, and he earned extra money doing before-and-after portraits for a local orthodontist. I can still clearly remember looking in the washing tray at the floating, disembodied mouths of the children with lips stretched, displaying their crooked teeth or showing off their newly straightened ones.

I began to photograph seriously in 1975, documenting the life of my daughter and the extended family I was forming in Berkeley. I had lost my job at UC Berkeley, was living on welfare, and desperately needed a roommate. My neighbors had photographic darkroom equipment but no place for it, so instead of a roommate I set up the equipment in my extra bedroom and taught myself how to print. I fell completely in love with photography. At thirty-five, in a moment of vision or foolishness or both, I decided that after ten years of teaching literature and writing, photography would be my life. Friends counseled otherwise, admonishing that I was being reckless and that photographers were a dime a dozen. How was I going to switch careers, especially with no formal training or resources? But I was hardheaded and persistent, making photos during the day and spending entire nights in the darkroom, printing photos over and over and over again.

The following year, a jazz drummer friend, Bob, invited me to hear some music in San Francisco. I opened the door to Keystone Korner and walked into what felt like Manhattan. The jazz club was small and dark, and the sounds coming from the bandstand – the honks, the cries, the sirens of the streets, the confinement and freedom of New York – rushed at me with such force that I stood in the doorway as though rooted to the floor. Home. I didn't even realize how homesick I had been.

When we went back the next week to hear Elvin Jones, Bob introduced me to Keystone's owner, Todd Barkan. In his inimitable and insistent way, Bob told Todd that I should be allowed to photograph in the club, and Todd agreed. The arrangement was that I could come in whenever I wanted, without paying, as long as I gave Todd a print of whomever I photographed. It was an incredible offer – a gift, really. Elvin Jones was the first musician I photographed, and for the next seven years, I spent two or three nights a week at the club. I wouldn't have been able to do that if Keystone Korner hadn't been, as the musicians described it, "a family kind of place." I often brought my daughter with me and she was always welcomed. When she wasn't helping collect tickets with the door people, who adored her, she was hanging out with the musicians or sleeping in the backroom.

The light was atrocious in Keystone Korner. Overhead spots made hot light on the protruding planes of the musicians' faces and cut deep shadows in their eyes. I learned my craft by looking at highlights and dark places. Sometimes, a musician would sit or stand in the center hot spot, and then I would search his or her face, although for the most part those opportunities were rare.

The overall lighting was flat and dim. I can still remember setting my camera to f/1.4 (wide open, no depth of field) and one-thirtieth of a second (a very slow shutter speed), which meant that my focus would be off if my hand shook the slightest bit. Photographing more than one player and keeping them in sharp focus meant that they had to be on the same plane, which rarely happened. It was a photographer's nightmare, but I was too inexperienced to sweat it. I just worked with what I had, and I learned more about the effects of light and the limits of film than I ever would have in a classroom.

Early on I began a series of jazz photographs where the face of the musician ceased to be central. By doing so, the musician's body language and his relationship to his instrument intensified the feeling of passion and energy that I was experiencing and trying to translate onto film. I wanted to capture both the rush of being in the moment and the power of the people creating music onstage, those great artists who were telling us all about freedom.

Quite frequently, I'd run into another photographer, Tom Copi (I think he went every night), but we had such different shooting styles that we never got in each other's way. I sat up front and used wide-angle and normal lenses; I was *in* the music. And I'd move around, shooting from the side and back of the stage, as well as from a few other spots in the club's very limited area. Tom, on the other hand, shot from the back with a long lens. Personally, he was much closer to Todd than I was and sometimes was allowed to come in early and move around the lights. Keystone was very much a man's world and I felt that I needed to be fairly invisible if I was to succeed with my work. Sometimes, Todd would stop and speak, but mostly he ignored me. Years later, when I was making photographs of women giving birth, this ability to be invisible was invaluable.

The mural on the back wall of Keystone's stage provided another photographic problem: visually noisy and psychedelic, the painting made it impossible to get a clean, uncluttered shot of anyone at the back of the stage. The musicians, especially the bass players, merged with the mural to the point where it seemed to become a part of their music, and that became part of the design of the photographs. The mirror to the right of the stage posed another set of problems. I loved shooting musicians in the mirror and on the stage at the same time, but I could rarely get both images in focus because there wasn't enough light. Occasionally, if the players were positioned in just the right way, it worked. In fact, for all the lighting problems, the Keystone's tiny stage allowed me to catch the interactions between the musicians; in no other club was I able to photograph the horn player listening to the piano player (with both of them in the image), or the bass player smiling at a drum solo.

I wanted to be taken seriously as a photographer and not be considered merely a groupie in Keystone Korner, and to that end I established a routine that kept me in good stead with the musicians. I knew the ways in which black musicians had been disrespected – terribly used and abused – and I didn't want to contribute to that. So I would go to the club on Tuesday night, when the band opened its week-long stay, listen to the music, introduce myself, and ask the band's permission to make photographs. The musicians seemed genuinely pleased that I sought their consent, and nobody ever refused me.

On Thursday, I would return to Keystone to photograph, and on Sunday, the last night of each engagement, I'd bring prints for each of the musicians, as well as one for Todd Barkan. I developed fine, long-lasting friendships with many of the artists, and I had a few wonderfully intense love affairs along the way (despite promising myself that I would not get involved with these magical musicians).

My one regret is that I didn't tape the stories I was privy to as I sat in the backroom between and after sets, listening to the musicians talk with each other. It took me a while to understand the import of what I was hearing, but even then I knew I couldn't manage a tape recorder *and* a camera.

What I learned was that to make this music of improvisation demands a highly imaginative and creative mind, not only to blow, but also to live a life that enables one to make the music. The backroom was where the elders taught the youngsters the things they'd need to know in addition to mouthpieces and harmony. How they'd need to step around disharmony or become their own mouthpieces when a club owner refused to pay them or when their bus was stuck in an Iowa snowstorm and they couldn't call AAA. Embedded in the musicians' tales that evoked knowing laughter were the tools for hammering together an improvised life. You couldn't make the music and survive without this knowledge, and those lessons didn't come in school or in books – they came from the stories shared in clubs' backrooms and on the back seats of buses during the long nights the itinerant musicians traveled in order to make a living. Keystone was, for all the musicians, a home and a haven.

One night, I walked backstage to greet Art Blakey shortly after the band completed its first set. The band members were sitting and standing with their heads down, metaphorically shuffling their feet, looking like young boys in the principal's office. The tension in the usually relaxed space was thick. Blakey was reading the young musicians the riot act about how to present oneself onstage. He was particularly aggrieved that some of the horn players had retreated to the back of the stage or offstage after their solos. He talked about deportment and respect for the audience, and their role as messengers of the music. He was teaching and preaching the gospel of jazz.

Art Blakey was one of the few musicians who, when I first met him, turned to me and asked, "And who are you? What do you do?" So I invited him for Sunday dinner. Ayisha was seven at the time and we lived in a small house in North Oakland. Although we had a little table in our eat-in kitchen, we had no dining room table and minimal living room furniture. No matter. Blakey came and sat with me in the kitchen while I cooked, and Ayisha brought out her violin and sat in his lap and played for him. It was like having my father there with us. Later on, band members and friends came by, and we all sat around on the floor and ate fried chicken and rice and greens. Art Blakey later told me that this was the first time an American had invited him home for dinner. I suggested that he must be exaggerating, but he swore that all over the world people had invited him home for a meal, but I was the first in the USA. I loved him saying that, but I never quite believed him.

Early on, we discovered that we were both great literature fans, and after that, whenever we met, we always talked about what we were reading, how his son and my daughter were faring, and why I wasn't moving to New York where he thought I needed to be. He offered several times to take Ayisha to live with his family out on Long Island so that I could hang out in Manhattan and make photographs of the music. I loved his bigness of spirit.

Blakey's pleasure at having been invited for dinner led me to continue that practice with other musicians. One evening after dinner, as Oliver Lake and I sat in my living room, he made a halfhearted pass at me. I commented gently that I had invited him for dinner but not for breakfast. He cracked up, and then apologized very earnestly, telling me that most women who invited musicians home for dinner expected to be "paid back" with sex. He told me how relieved he was, and I managed not to be offended at his relief. I understood that he was offering a lesson. He and I were friends for many years, shared numerous home-cooked dinners, and maintained deep respect for one another.

I did come to jazz with the important men in my life, but during my years at Keystone Korner, I made the music my own. Those years between 1976 and 1983, when Keystone Korner closed, were certainly challenging: I was developing my craft and struggling to make a living, just as so many of the musicians were struggling. But the nights at Keystone Korner nourished us all. I hope and trust that this music that feeds our souls will continue to swing in dark corners with low lights.

In Memoriam:
Ronnie Matthews (1935–2008)
John Ross (1938–2011)
Helen Wray (1951–2010)
Eddie Marshall (1938–2011)

Ayisha and Art, 1977

ACKNOWLEDGMENTS

This book began in my photographs. Looking through hundreds of images, I came to feel that the Keystone Korner story needed many voices in order to give a fuller, rounder picture – a "talkie" instead of a silent film. Striving to get as many viewpoints about Keystone as possible, I had lengthy, taped conversations with people who had various relationships with the club: the musicians, the club's staff, the club's owner, and audience members. I started each session with "Tell me about Keystone." As we shared stories, I would sometimes circle back to a thought or an idea for elaboration or occasionally nudge a memory back on track, but basically I followed the storytellers' tunes. I have learned through photographing people that if you allow them to be comfortable in their bodies rather than direct them into poses, the portraits are truer. It is the same with interviews. Conversations work better. Memories are tricky business. There are bound to be discrepancies when folks think back twenty-five years. For all the storytellers in this book, myself included, we are remembering not only a place and a time, but also our youth. As George Cables said when he looked at the photographs, "We were all thin. We all had more hair." We were all young, though some more than others. Jesse "Chuy" Varella (the music director at KCSM, a Bay Area jazz station) referred to himself and the other very young listeners and musicians as "the Keystone Kids."

I conceived of the chapters in musical terms: some are structured like big band arrangements, with many storytellers; others are more like quartets and solos. My role is best described by Mike Thelwell, who crafted Stokely Carmichael's (Kwame Ture) biography, *Ready for Revolution*, from taped conversations. He said, "The formulation which seems to me most accurate comes from music: Kwame being the composer and I the arranger."

It's difficult to know where to begin the long list of acknowledgments that are due to all the people who contributed to this collective musical memoir. Do I start in the present, when I began orchestrating it, or do I begin at the beginning, when I first started photographing at Keystone Korner? Or the beginning before that, when, for my eighth or ninth birthday, my parents gave me my first Brownie box camera? The

209

hierarchy of lists also concerns me. All of the people who contributed to my growth as a photographer, who provided unstinting friendship and love, and who were so bighearted in their help with this particular endeavor are truly at the top, no matter where they fall on the list. With these caveats and in roughly chronological order, then, I first thank my parents, Perry and Neddie Sloane, who always encouraged me to be myself, and my daughter, Ayisha, my heart, for keeping me centered, loving me unconditionally, and enduring years of my photographing her every move. Thank you also, Ayisha, for accompanying me to Keystone Korner on so many nights and uncomplainingly sleeping on the backroom couch. For contributing to my growth as a photographer, I must thank Jean Doak and Carl Anthony for giving me a complete darkroom shortly after I moved next door to them in 1972. Special thanks to Jean for teaching me the rudiments of photographic printing. I thank Lewis Watts for letting me sit in on his photography class at UC Berkeley and for encouraging me to follow my passion for photography when everyone else thought I was crazy to give up teaching. And I thank Todd Barkan for allowing me free access to Keystone Korner, asking only for prints in return. I am especially grateful for the blessings he has given to this book. Thank you to cherished friends Renee Smith Boone and Maria Rosa Keys for keeping me company and exploring the music with me without getting irritated when I disappeared into the backroom of the club. I am particularly grateful to Maria Rosa for checking in on me constantly and dragging me out into the sunshine during my long periods of reclusiveness while I was working on this book. My deep thanks go to Kunle Mwanga for kick-starting *Keystone Korner: Portrait of a Jazz Club* by casually suggesting, in the spring of 2006, that I make a book of my Keystone photographs. Kunle went through all my Keystone contact sheets and was invaluable in identifying people and giving feedback on image choices. Boundless gratitude goes to all the storytellers in *Keystone Korner: Portrait of a Jazz Club*, who were beyond gracious. For our conversations, they invited me to their homes or came to mine in Oakland or Tracy Collins's home in Brooklyn; they met me in restaurants or backstage at clubs. Todd Barkan invited me to Dizzy's Club Coca Cola, sat with me for hours talking about Keystone, and then comped me for the show!

The generosity of spirit that was so much a part of Keystone Korner suffuses this book. Thank you to Arthur Monroe, who educated me in the history and culture of jazz, and gave me the gift of his love for Bird. My deep appreciation to valued friends Nadine Wilmot and Maxine

Craig for schooling me on the methodology of oral histories and to Stuart Kremsky, who voluntarily assembled the Keystone discography. Cheers go to Reggie Major for lending me his old transcription machine, to Brian Auerbach for resuscitating one of my broken tapes, and to Sammy Wooten for lending me his laptop so I could work in front of the living room heater when my studio was too cold to bear. Thank you to Helen Wray for sharing her invaluable collection of Keystone memorabilia and to Allen Pittman, who mailed me the original IRS notice which was nailed to the door of Keystone Korner, shuttering it forever.

Tracy Collins's kindness has contributed to my life in myriad ways. He videotaped my interviews in New York, provided his guest room when I was there, and when I needed a retreat, he offered his home for several weeks and left me to my work. His love, constant encouragement, and critical eye continue to enrich me. Thank you to my dear friend Karla Brundage for reading draft after draft of my own essay and for patiently helping me shape it by asking all the right questions. I can't thank her enough for her continuing love and support.

Having long admired his writing on music, I knew early on that I wanted Al Young to write the preface. Al mentored this project from the beginning, checked in regularly to cheer me on, and wrote a magnificent overview of the Bay Area jazz scene. For all of this and for connecting me with Sascha Feinstein, I thank him profusely. Sascha deserves his own book of thank yous. In the spring of 2008 he published my essay "My Years at Keystone" along with eight of my jazz photos in *Brilliant Corners: A Journal of Jazz and Literature*, which he edits. As our friendship deepened, he succumbed to my constant pleas that he co-edit this book, a gift I can never repay. Sascha later hosted me at his home in Pennsylvania so that we could select photos together, and it was he who introduced the book to Indiana University Press, with which he had already published four books on jazz. His enthusiasm for and meticulous, respectful editing of *Keystone Korner* made it a much better book. A big thank you also goes to Marleni, Sascha's brilliant and beautiful wife, for her warm hospitality, and to their children, Kiran and Divia, who welcomed me into their family.

There is no proper way to thank friends who read first or second or final drafts of a book. Much love goes to Maxine and Mitch Craig and to Veronica Selver. The Craigs read my entire first draft, and Maxine gave me pages of invaluable feedback. Veronica read a late draft and gave me reams of marvelous suggestions that I used to strengthen the final version of the text. Thank you to Julius Lester for years of marvelous discussions about photography and writing, as well as his insightful questions and critiques on the text and images in this work. I am indebted to him for his sage advice on negotiating the publishing process. Thank you to Hank O'Neal and Nat Hentoff for their enthusiastic pre-publication support. Thanks also to David Rife for copyediting the final draft.

As I approached my deadline, I spent weeks shuffling photos and obsessing over their placement in the final layout. Needing fresh eyes, I asked three friends with different skill sets for critical feedback. My love and deep appreciation go to these women, consummate problem solvers all, for their perfect suggestions: Anita Carse, Pauline Wynter, and again Veronica Selver.

Indiana University Press has been a joy to work with. Thanks to Jane Behnken for her keen interest in this book on first hearing about it; for shepherding it through publication; for her patience with my need to micromanage; and for giving me more creative control than I ever hoped for. Sarah Wyatt Swanson, Bernadette Zoss, Daniel Pyle, Robert Sloan, Peter Froehlich, and Angela Burton have been available and helpful at every turn. Special thanks go to Jamison Cockerham for the overall design of the book and its cover and for ensuring the photographs sing. Very special thanks to my copyeditor, Merryl Sloane (no relation), for her thoroughness, delicate touch, and hand-holding. Her kindness and patience truly saved my sanity during the editing process. My gratitude to all of you.

Finally, for asking just often enough, "How's the book coming?" and for constant encouragement, I offer unending thanks to the following friends. If I have left anyone off this list, I apologize: Donna Andrews, Scott Barton, Daphne Bogart, Denise Bradley, Anthony Brown, Penelope Collins, Rachel Crystal, Jacques Depelchin, Cheryl Fabio, Jim Fleming, Cheryl Garrett, David Henderson, Shabaka Henley, Mildred Howard, Lewanne Jones, Calvin Keys, Stephanie Knight-Shaw, Michele Mason, Clairmonte Moore, John Moore, Daphne Muse, Angela Johnson Peters, Kathryn Takara, Lydia Tanji, Michele Washington, Jean Wiley, Sherri Willis, and Marianne Yang.

Acknowledgments

**Compiled by
Stuart Kremsky**

Nat Adderley. *Blue Autumn*, Theresa T R 122 (Oct. 28, 1982)

———. *On the Move*, Theresa T R 117 (Oct. 28, 1982)

Chet Baker. *Sings, Plays, Live at the Keystone Korner*, HighNote H C D 7112 (Jan. 12, 1978)

Art Blakey and the Jazz Messengers. *In This Korner*, Concord Jazz C J-68 (May 8, 1978)

———. *Straight Ahead*, Concord Jazz C J-168, C C D-4168 (June 1981)

———. *Keystone 3*, Concord Jazz C J-196, C C D-4196 (Jan. 1982)

Jaki Byard. *Sunshine of My Soul: Live at the Keystone Korner*, HighNote H C D 7169 (1978)

George Cables. *Morning Song*, HighNote H C D 7182 (1980)

Steve Cohn. *Sufi Dancers*, White Cow W C R 1201 (Jan. 25, 1982)

Paquito D'Rivera. *Live at Keystone Korner*, CBS (Europe) 25657 (June 17–18, 1983)

Bill Evans Trio. *Consecration*, Alfa Jazz (Japan) O O R 2-61-68; reissued as Milestone 8 M C D-4430 (8-C D boxed set, Aug. 31–Sept. 7, 1980)

———. *The Last Waltz*, Milestone 8 M C D-4436 (8-C D boxed set, Aug. 31–Sept. 7, 1980)

Red Garland Trio. *Groovin' Live*, Alfa Jazz (Japan) A L C R 97/98 (Mar. 7, 8, 11, 12, 1974)

———. *Groovin' Live II*, Alfa Jazz (Japan) A L C R 102/103 (Mar. 7, 8, 11, 12, 1974)

———. *Keystones!*, Xanadu (Japan) C R C J-5009 (May 12, 1977)

———. *I Left My Heart . . .*, Muse M R 5311; reissued on C D as *32 Jazz* 32107 (May 1978)

Stan Getz Quartet. *The Dolphin*, Concord Jazz C J-158 (May 10, 1981)

———. *Spring Is Here*, Concord Jazz C C D-4500 (May 1981) (Both Stan Getz records were released as a 2-C D set, *My Old Flame*.)

Dexter Gordon Quartet. *Nights at the Keystone 1–3*, Blue Note C D P 7-94848/50 (May 13, 1978–Mar. 27, 1979) (All three volumes are collected in Mosaic Select 14.)

Eddie Harris. *Tale of Two Cities*, Night 91589 (1978)

Tom Hoffman. *Live at Keystone Korner* (prob. 1982)

Freddie Hubbard. *Classics*, Fantasy F-9635 (Nov. 28, 1981)

———. *Keystone Bop*, Fantasy F-9615 (Nov. 29, 1981)

———. *A Little Night Music*, Fantasy F-9626 (Nov. 29, 1981) (These three albums were reconstituted as *Keystone Bop: Sunday Night*, Prestige P R C D-24146; and *Keystone Bop, Vol. 2: Friday/Saturday*, Prestige P R C D-24163.)

———. *Above & Beyond*, Metropolitan M R 1113 (June 17, 1982)

Bobby Hutcherson. *Farewell Keystone*, Theresa T R 124, Evidence E C D 22018 (July 10–11, 1982)

Lee Katzman Quartet. *Naptown Reunion*, 25th Century Ensemble (June 23, 1980)

Rahsaan Roland Kirk. *The Man Who Cried Fire*, Night 2-91592 (mid-1970s)

———. *Bright Moments*, Atlantic S D 2-907, Rhino R 2-72409 (June 8–9, 1973)

Yusef Lateef. *10 Years Hence*, Atlantic S D 2-1001 (July 5, 1974)

Dave Liebman and Richie Beirach. *Mosaic Select*, Mosaic Select 12 (disk 1 only, 1976)

Charles Mingus Quintet. *Keystone Korner*, Jazz Door (Italy) 1219 (Apr. 1976)

Tete Montoliu. *Live at the Keystone Korner*, Timeless (Holland) S J P-138 (Sept. 28–29, 1979)

Art Pepper. *San Francisco Samba*, Contemporary C C D-14086 (Aug. 6–8, 1977)

Pharoah Sanders. *Heart Is a Melody*, Theresa T R 118 (Jan. 23, 1982)

Woody Shaw. *Live Volume One*, HighNote H C D 7031 (1977)

———. *Live Volume Two*, HighNote H C D 7089 (late 1970s)

———. *Live Volume Three*, HighNote HCD 7102 (1977)

———. *Live Volume Four*, HighNote HCD 7139 (fall 1981)

Zoot Sims. *On the Korner*, Pablo PACD-2310-953 (Mar. 20, 1983)

Jimmy Smith and Eddie Harris. *All the Way Live*, Milestone MCD-9251 (Aug. 23, 1981)

Sonny Stitt. *Just in Case You Forgot How Bad He Really Was*, 32 Jazz 32051 (Sept. 1981)

Timeless All-Stars. *It's Timeless*, Timeless SJP178, CDSJP178 (Apr. 28, 1982)

McCoy Tyner. *Atlantis*, Milestone 55002, MCD-55002 (Aug. 31–Sept. 1, 1974)

Eddie "Cleanhead" Vinson. *Redux: Live at the Keystone Korner*, Savant SCD2052 (Jan. 13, 1979)

Cedar Walton. *Among Friends*, Theresa TRCD129, Evidence ECD-22023 (July 1982)

Mary Lou Williams. *Live at the Keystone Korner*, HighNote HCD 7097 (May 8, 1977)

Denny Zeitlin and Charlie Haden. *Time Remembers One Time Once*, ECM 1239 (July 1981)

Sascha Feinstein

"There's just too much great music," I said to Todd Barkan in a recent conversation about this Keystone CD. "I'm going to have to make some serious sacrifices." Todd paused, taking it in, and then concurred: "Yeah, there's *a lot* of good stuff." Just as attempting a "definitive," single-disk compilation of recordings from the Village Vanguard would be preposterous, compiling a sampling of Keystone Korner sessions inevitably results in major omissions. Still, as an introduction, what's here honors the talent that blessed Keystone during its eleven years. Rahsaan Roland Kirk, McCoy Tyner, Woody Shaw, Dexter Gordon, Bill Evans, Stan Getz, Cedar Walton, Bobby Hutcherson, Art Blakey, Wynton Marsalis – for those who love jazz, the names alone carry a magisterial weight.

Who's most obviously missing? We can start with two albums, both titled *Live at the Keystone Korner*: one led by Mary Lou Williams, recorded on her sixty-seventh birthday (HighNote), and one by Tete Montoliu, a personal favorite (Timeless). Art Pepper recorded *San Francisco Samba* (Contemporary) in 1977, a fine concert coming right on the heels of his Village Vanguard triumph; his quartet included drummer Eddie Marshall, one of the club's mainstays, as well as another Keystone keystone: pianist George Cables, Pepper's musical soulmate, whom he dubbed "Mr. Beautiful." Cables, of course, appears on this CD with Dexter Gordon, but I'd also like to plug his 1980 solo/quartet album *Morning Song* (HighNote). Nat Adderley, Chet Baker, Jaki Byard, Red Garland, Freddie Hubbard, Yusef Lateef, Charles Mingus, Zoot Sims, Jimmy Smith, Sonny Stitt, Eddie "Cleanhead" Vinson – one really needs a Keystone boxed set. Such recordings – and so many others! – should supplement this sampler in order to more completely support the photographs and oral histories in this book and, more generally, to experience the joys of the live performances.

That disclaimer aside, the enclosed compilation includes some of the most important musicians in the history of modern jazz and starts, appropriately, with one of Todd Barkan's guiding spirits: Rahsaan Roland Kirk, whose concerts became legendary for their transformative effervescence. Although six cuts from *The Man Who Cried Fire* feature Rahsaan at Keystone, a more complete concert experience can be heard on *Bright Moments*, the two-CD set recorded in 1973. When I mentioned to Todd that my favorite cut from *Bright Moments* was **"Jitterbug Waltz,"** he said, "Rahsaan would be pleased with that. That was one of his favorites from the gig." Man, he made my day.

The next selection's an emotional workout: the McCoy Tyner Quartet muscling through a rendition of his composition **"Pursuit."** This 1974 cut from *Atlantis* presents Tyner's only recording of the tune. Somewhat reminiscent of Coltrane's "Pursuance" from *A Love Supreme* – with its introductory drum statement and high energy, further propelled by the Coltrane-inspired virtuosity of tenor saxophonist Azar Lawrence – "Pursuit" makes serious demands on the listener. To quote Neil Tesser, "'Pursuit' remains as densely populated with ideas, textures, and technique as almost anything Tyner had recorded up till then."

Trumpeter Woody Shaw recorded four Keystone CDs, all titled *Live* and released on the HighNote label. Three of the four include trombonist Steve Turre, an important voice in this book, including the third volume of *Live*, from which we get this spicy rendition of Shaw's **"Ginseng People."** It's possible that the leader had some pangs for the opposite coast (before the theme-break tag, he gives a wink to "There's a Boat That's Leaving Soon for New York") but, on this cut and all others, he's absolutely *present*. Can one spend considerable time lamenting Woody Shaw's anonymity in America's collective consciousness? Of course. But it's better to pass along the music.

Most of the tunes covered by Dexter Gordon and his quartet on the three volumes titled *Nights at the Keystone* run over twelve minutes; some last nearly twenty. Experienced individually (as released by Blue Note) or collectively (as released by Mosaic), these near-mythic performances illuminate an on-the-stand, evolving relationship. As producer Michael Cuscuna said, "The chemistry among these four men was immediately apparent and growing each day. Dexter Gordon moved from star soloist to bandleader, shaping a magnificent quartet." I would add that the quartet played marvelously right from the start, and **"Antabus,"** a composition named for the anti-drug medicine and featured on the first volume, testifies to that claim.

Of all the artists to record at Keystone Korner, none has been more thoroughly documented than pianist Bill Evans with his final trio, featuring Marc Johnson on bass and Joe La Barbera on drums. Each of his boxed sets – *The Last Waltz* and *Consecration*, both subtitled *The Final*

Recordings – contains eight CDs. Experiencing the totality of either set requires an indulgence that we rarely, if ever, permit in our lives. Selecting just one of the 133 cuts would have been overwhelming except that a "bad" choice was nearly impossible; the sets include stunningly fine performances, despite the fact that Evans would die just days later. This version of **"Polka Dots and Moonbeams"** highlights the trio's symbiosis, a connective awareness that almost defies simile.

Tenor saxophonist Stan Getz cut two Keystone LPs in 1981, *The Dolphin* and *Spring Is Here*, each later released individually on CD and then collectively on the twofer *My Old Flame*. True of each performance, this version of **"Joy Spring"** presents Getz sounding completely at ease, releasing long, fluid phrases that float above and within a supportive and inspiring rhythm section: Lou Levy on piano, Monty Budwig on bass, and Victor Lewis on drums. Levy and Getz first played together in Woody Herman's band in 1948, and Levy joined Getz's quartet in the late '50s. But these sessions from '81 marked their first reunion since 1959; they also represent the only recordings by this particular, marvelous quartet.

Vibraphonist Bobby Hutcherson, unquestionably one of the club favorites, recorded with Freddie Hubbard and Joe Henderson at the Keystone in 1981, and those all-star jams can be heard on two Prestige volumes under Hubbard's leadership, both titled *Keystone Bop*. The following year, Hutcherson released his own album, *Farewell Keystone*, using a sextet that included the Cedar Walton trio. And later that year, when Walton returned to record *Among Friends*, Hutcherson joined in for **"My Foolish Heart,"** a special feature and a true highlight. Speaking about the Keystone identity, Todd Barkan once wrote, "No musician in the world better personified the spirit and sensitivity of that special musical environment than did vibraharpist and composer Bobby Hutcherson." This cut speaks to that praise.

The legendary drummer Art Blakey recorded three albums at Keystone, one in 1978, *In This Korner*; another in '81, *Straight Ahead*; and a final one in the following year, appropriately titled *Keystone 3*, which includes **"In Walked Bud."** In addition to Billy Pierce on tenor, Donald Brown on piano, and Charles Fambrough on bass, this incarnation of Blakey's Messengers featured the Marsalis brothers: Wynton on trumpet and Branford on alto. Blakey had recorded with the brothers before (in 1980) and with each individually, but this Keystone session would be their last recorded outing with the drum master. At the time of this gig, Branford was twenty-one; Wynton, who energizes the bridge with

Ellingtonian growls, was twenty. Throughout, Blakey ignites his young lions with dramatic textures and rhythmic propulsion.

"In Walked Bud" concludes with a false ending that plays with and to the audience: the horns cadence, but the piano continues the theme – and then stops mid-phrase, leaving everyone hanging. The applause and collective murmuring might translate to "Okay, I guess that *is* it." And on some level, at least, that seems a fitting close for this CD. From all accounts, few could accept the closure of Keystone – yet the music and the stories keep the doors if not fully open then somewhat ajar. As Amiri Baraka writes at the end of his poem "In Walked Bud": "In walked *us*."

Recordings on Keystone Korner: Portrait of a Jazz Club CD

1. "Jitterbug Waltz" (T. Fats Waller)   7:05
   (Chappell & Co.)
   Rahsaan Roland Kirk, *Bright Moments* (1973)
   Rahsaan Roland Kirk (stritch), Ron Burton (p),
   Henry Pearson (b), Robert Shy (d), Joe Habao (perc)

2. "Pursuit" (M. Tyner)   9:21
   (Aisha Music)
   McCoy Tyner, *Atlantis* (1974)
   McCoy Tyner (p), Azar Lawrence (tenor), Joony
   Booth (b), Wilby Fletcher (d), Guilherme Franco (perc)

3. "Ginseng People" (W. Shaw)   11:39
   (Celestial Harmonies)
   Woody Shaw, *Live: Volume 3* (1977)
   Woody Shaw (trp), Steve Turre (tbn), Mulgrew
   Miller (p), Stafford James (b), Victor Lewis (d)

4. "Antabus" (D. Gordon)   7:43
   (Dex Music, Inc.)
   Dexter Gordon, *Nights at the Keystone, Volume 1* (1978)
   Dexter Gordon (tenor), George Cables (p),
   Rufus Reid (b), Eddie Gladden (d)

5. "Polka Dots and Moonbeams" (J. Van Heusen, J. Burke)   5:03
   (Marke Music/My Dad's Songs/Reganesque Music/
   Bourne Co./Limerick Music)
   Bill Evans, *The Last Waltz* (1980)
   Bill Evans (p), Marc Johnson (b), Joe La Barbera (d)

6. "Joy Spring" (C. Brown)   9:44
   (Second Floor Music)
   Stan Getz, *The Dolphin* (1981)
   Stan Getz (tenor), Lou Levy (p), Monty Budwig (b),
   Victor Lewis (d)

7. "My Foolish Heart" (V. Young, N. Washington)   11:57
   (Patti Washington Music/Catharine Hinen Music/
   Chappell & Co.)
   Cedar Walton, *Among Friends* (1982)
   Cedar Walton (p), Bobby Hutcherson (vibes),
   Buster Williams (b), Billy Higgins (d)

8. "In Walked Bud" (T. Monk)   8:26
   (Embassy Music Corp.)
   Art Blakey, *Keystone 3* (1982)
   Art Blakey (d), Wynton Marsalis (trp), Branford Marsalis
   (alto), Donald Brown (p), Charles Fambrough (b)

KATHY SLOANE has been a freelance photographer for thirty-five years and has exhibited her jazz images in San Francisco, Oakland, and Los Angeles. In New York, she exhibited along with bassist-photographer Milt Hinton. A portfolio of her work was featured in *JazzTimes,* and five of her images appeared in Ken Burns's PBS documentary *Jazz.*

SASCHA FEINSTEIN is Professor of English at Lycoming College and founding editor of *Brilliant Corners: A Journal of Jazz & Literature.* He was awarded the 2008 Pennsylvania Governor's Award for Artist of the Year and the Hayden Carruth Award for his poetry collection *Misterioso.* He lives in Williamsport, Pennsylvania.

Helen Humes, 1977